Name _____

My Reading Strategy Guide

When I **predict/infer**, do I . . .

Look at the pictures?	☐
Think about what I know?	☐
Make a guess about what will happen?	☐

When I **think about words**, do I . . .

Try to sound out words I don't know?	☐
Try to see how the words are used in the story?	☐

When I **self-question**, do I . . .

Ask questions to answer for myself as I read along?	☐
Look at the pictures for clues?	☐

When I **monitor**, do I . . .

Stop and ask if I understand the story?	☐
Reread?	☐
Read ahead?	☐
Look at the pictures for clues?	☐
Ask for help?	☐

When I **evaluate**, do I . . .

See how I feel about what I read?	☐
Ask if I like what I read?	☐

When I **summarize**, do I . . .

Think about the parts of the story—the beginning, the middle, and the end?	☐
Summarize as I read and after I read?	☐

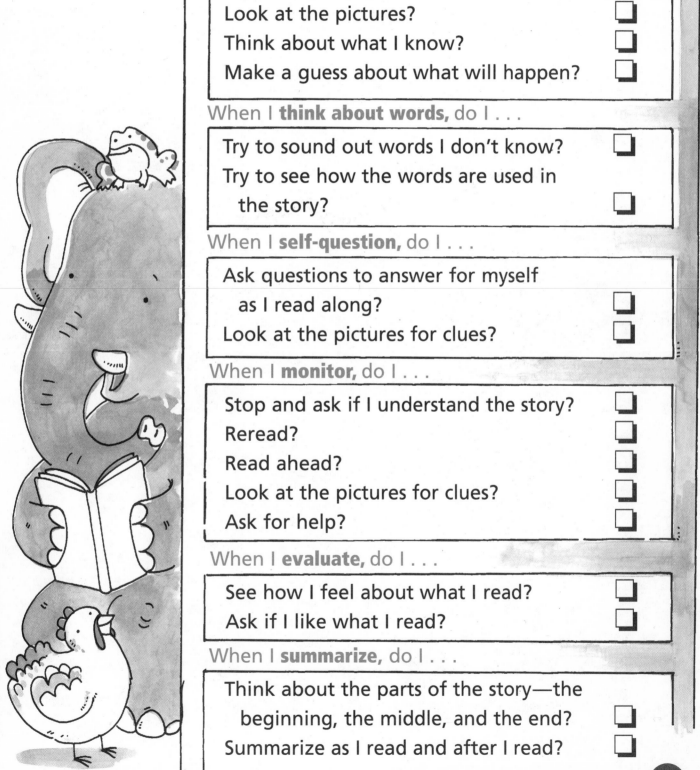

The Writing Process

Prewriting

- Choose an idea to write about.
- Plan your writing.

Drafting

- Write about your idea.
- Don't worry about mistakes.

Revising

- Read what you have written.
- Is there anything you want to add?
- Is there anything you want to change?

Proofreading

- Check your spelling.
- Check to see that your sentences are complete.

Publishing and Sharing

- Think of a good title.
- Make a clean copy of your writing.
- Find a way to share your writing with others.

Name

Let's Get Started!

What are you going to write about yourself?

Draw or write your ideas in the circles.

What I'll Tell
About Me

Name

Take Another Look

• Revising Checklist •

Answer these questions about your writing.

☐ Have I told enough?

☐ Is there anything I should add?

☐ Is there anything I should change?

Changes I Want to Make:

_____

_____

Questions to Ask My Writing Partner

- What do you like best about what I have written?
- Is there anything I need to add?
- Is there anything I should change?

Name John Thomas

A Cat Tale

Read this story about Shadow's new life. Then fill in the story map.

Shadow's Kittens

Shadow and her kittens lived in the quiet van. One day a dog jumped in the van. The kittens ran away. Shadow looked until she found them. She took the kittens to the turkey shed. They will be safe there.

Setting	Characters
Van	

Problem
A dog jumped in the van and scared the kittens away.

Event 1	Shadow took the kittens
Event 2	to the turkey shed and they were all safe.
Event 3	

Ending

Name

Tongue Twister Cats

Finish each tongue twister. Use a word
that begins like the underlined word
and rhymes with the word at the end.

1 <u>Cl</u>eo cleans clams with her _____. (jaws)

2 <u>St</u>ripes the stray strolls the _____ all day. (feet)

3 Friendly <u>Fr</u>ed _____ fresh fish on Fridays. (ties)

4 <u>Sn</u>owball snatches snails for a _____. (back)

5 <u>Tr</u>ix gets trapped climbing a tree _____. (junk)

6 <u>Br</u>enda brings Brian a brush and _____. (zoom)

7 Sleepy <u>Sl</u>oopy slides down a slippery _____. (hope)

Write your own tongue twister about a cat named
Stella. Use these words: **Stella, stares, stars**.

8 _____

_____

_____

Name ....

Missing Cats

Cut out and paste the cats where they belong in the picture.

My family has lost three cats. We left the door open, and they ran out. We hope they haven't gone too far. Where can they be?

It sits in a tree.

It rests quietly by a tree.

It is at the end of the street.

Pet Show Today!

11

Make a poster to help find a lost cat. Try to use the words **end**, **far**, **quietly**, **family**, **left**, and **street** on your poster.

Name _____

See the Sea

Some cats are off on an adventure. Use the picture clues and the words from the box to write the missing homonym pairs.

| sail   sale | eight   ate | blew   blue | rowed   road |

1 The boat with the red 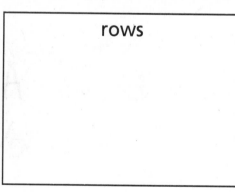 _____ is for

_____.

2 The wind _____ and the sky was

_____.

3 The hungry cats _____ the boat

to shore and ate dinner next to the _____.

4 The _____ cats _____ fish stew.

Draw your own pictures for this homonym pair.

rows	rose

Name

Who Is the New Pet?

Use words from the box to write sentences about the picture.

| basket |
| children |
| sleeping |
| yarn |
| mouse |
| family |
| string |
| reading |
| feather |
| mother |
| father |
| tickle |

I slip on the grod.
I Jump up.

Name John Thomas

Shadow's Song

Each Spelling Word begins or ends with a **consonant cluster**. A consonant cluster is two or more consonant letters whose sounds are blended together.

consonant clusters ➡ left,   just,   old

Spelling Words	
1. **left**	5. **slip**
2. **just**	6. **drove**
3. **stay**	7. **trip**
4. **old**	8. **glad**

 Your Own Words

Write the missing consonant clusters on the turkey shed to finish each Spelling Word. Then write the words you made.

1 ju____ ____ _juma_   5 ____ ____ip _slip_

2 ____ ____ove _drove_   6 le____ ____ _lefl_

3 o____ ____ _glad_   7 ____ ____ip _slip_

4 ____ ____ad _glad_   8 ____ ____ay _stay_

Write Spelling Words to answer the questions.

9 Which word begins with
   the first sound you hear in ? _____

10 Which word rhymes with **sad**? _____

Name

Spelling Spree

Write a Spelling Word for each clue.
Then use the letters in the boxes to write
what Shadow was.

Spelling Words	
1. **left**	5. **slip**
2. **just**	6. **drove**
3. **stay**	7. **trip**
4. **old**	8. **glad**

1 to slide on ice

2 the opposite of **right**

3 a vacation

4 happy

5 to be in one place

Secret Word: ___ ___ ___ ___ ___

Find and circle three Spelling Words that are wrong in
this journal entry. Then write each word correctly.

Friday   Today I found five cats. I
put the cats in my ould van. I drov
all night. There was jist one other
car on the road. The trip was long,
and I was glad to get home.

6 _____

7 _____

8 _____

Name

Under a Full Moon

Some cats got together one night. Write sentences to tell what each cat is doing.

Example: Ginger is hiding.

1 _____

2 _____

3 _____

4 _____

Write a sentence that tells what the cats will do next.

5 _____

Name

I Want a Job

Read what Mrs. Piper and Jeff say.
Then fill out the form.

Jeff: I want to take care of pets.

Mrs. Piper: I could use some help in
my business. Will you fill this out?

Jeff: Well, thank you.

PIPER'S PET CARE SHOP

Name _____

① Are you a responsible person? Write about one responsibility you

have at home or at school. _____

_____

② What do pets need at night? _____

③ What problems should you watch for when you take care of a dog?

_____

_____

④ Which one of these animals would you like to have as a pet:

a dog, a cat, a goldfish? Tell why. _____

_____

On a separate sheet of paper, draw a poster to advertise
Piper's Pet Care Shop. Tell why it's a great place for pets.

....

Making It Happen

Use what you know about **Arthur's Pet Business** to complete the story frame. Look back at the story for help.

Arthur wanted _____.

His parents said he would have to show he was

_____ first.

Arthur decided to _____.

Mrs. Wood asked Arthur to _____.

Just before Perky was to go home, _____.

In the end, Perky _____.

Draw a picture of what Arthur got at the end of the story.

Name

A Tiny Ball of Fur

Look at the pictures. Read each story. Then write
answers to the questions.

Miko grinned. She held out her
arms. A tiny ball of brown fur looked
up at her. Miko smiled and said, "Am
I dreaming? Is this really happening
to me?"

She kissed the furry ball and said,
"This is the best day of my life."

How did Miko feel? _____

How do you know? _____

Miko was standing at her front
door. She was yelling the same name
over and over. "Max! Where are
you?" Miko's eyes filled with tears.
She didn't know what to do.

How did Miko feel? _____

How do you know? _____

Ask Arthur

fish	fresh	much
splash	munch	trick

Use words from the box to finish each sentence.

Pet Show Daily

Ask Arthur

Dear Arthur,

My _____ likes to _____ in the water. What should I do?

Don't worry so _____. That sounds like a good

_____.

Dear Arthur,

For her snack, my pet mouse likes to _____ on cheese. Is this good for her?

Yes, it is! Just be sure it is _____.

Write a question that you would like to ask Arthur about an animal. Then write an answer Arthur might give.

Question: _____

_____

Answer: _____

Name _____

The Big Sneeze

Use all the words in the bird cage to
write an ending to the story.

care
night
thank
these
watch

Mrs. Wood started to feel a little
twitching in her nose. AHH CHOO! AHH CHOO!
she sneezed. "Oh, no," she cried. "I do not feel well. I am
catching a cold. What if Orville gets sick? Then I couldn't
take him to the pet show tomorrow."

Just then her big green parrot, Orville, started to
squawk. "Now you've done it! Now you've done it! No
prize for Orville."

Mrs. Wood paced back and forth across the living room.
"Oh dear," she cried. "What shall I do? I don't want Orville
to catch my cold." Then she stopped walking. She rushed
to the telephone and dialed Arthur's number.

"Hello, Arthur?"

_____

_____

_____

_____

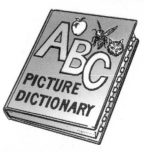

ABC Fun

Help Arthur write the missing letters on the pets.
Use ABC order.

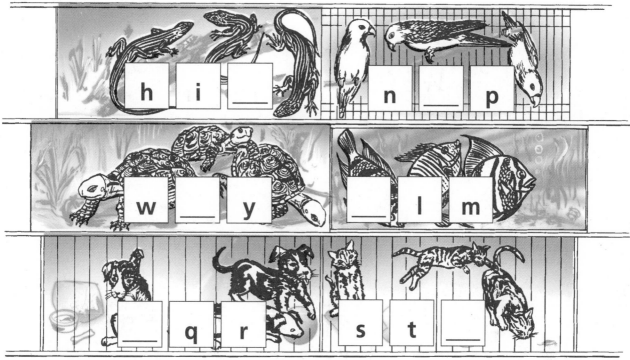

h   i   __   n   __   p

w   __   y   __   l   m

__   q   r   s   t   __

In which part of the dictionary would you find the following

animal names? Write **B**, **M**, **E** for beginning, middle, or end.

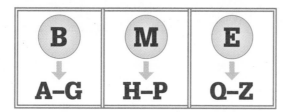

B	M	E
A–G	H–P	Q–Z

1 dog _____   4 ant _____   7 cat _____

2 rabbit _____   5 turtle _____   8 lizard _____

3 mouse _____   6 bird _____   9 skunk _____

Name

A Message for Sam

Write a phone message for Sam.
Use information from the picture.

I'm sorry, but Sam is
not home. This is
Kim. May I take a
message?

Yes, please. This is
Andrew. Will you ask
Sam to take his dog to
the park at 2:00? I want
to play catch with him.

WHILE YOU WERE OUT

To _____

Date _____ Time _____

Caller _____

Message _____

_____

_____

_____

Message taken by _____

24 Pet Show Today!

Name

A Wonderful Job

Each Spelling Word begins or ends with
the first sound you hear in or 🪑.

the sh sound ➜ she, dish

the ch sound ➜ chin, much

Spelling Words	
1. **dish**	5. **chin**
2. **she**	6. **wish**
3. **much**	7. **such**
4. **cash**	8. **chop**
📝 Your Own Words	

Write each Spelling Word on the suitcase
that has the matching **sh** or **ch** sound.

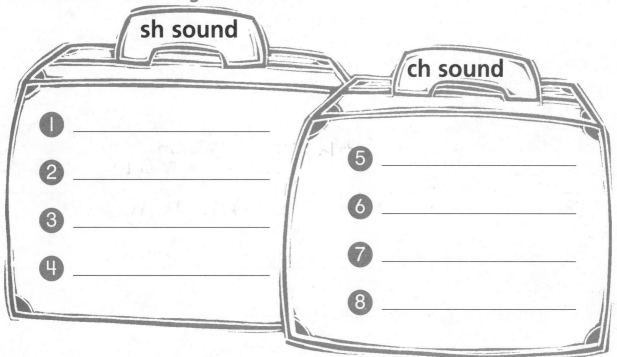

sh sound

1 _____

2 _____

3 _____

4 _____

ch sound

5 _____

6 _____

7 _____

8 _____

Write Spelling Words to answer the questions.

9 Which word begins with
the first sound you hear in ? _____

10 Which word begins with
the first sound you hear in ? _____

Name _____

Spelling Spree

Write a Spelling Word to finish the
second sentence in each pair.

1 The opposite of **boy** is **girl**.

The opposite of **he** is _____.

2 You **slice** a piece of **bread**.

You _____ a piece of wood.

3 You put **milk** in a **glass**.

You put **food** on a _____.

4 Your **toes** are part of your **foot**.

Your _____ is part of your **face**.

Find and circle four Spelling Words that are spelled wrong
in this ad. Then write each word correctly.

 Pet Care Today

Do you **wich** someone could watch your pet?
Then I am the person to call. I will take **sech**
good care of your pet. I do not charge too **mutch**.
You can pay me in **cass** or by check. HURRY!
You get a free pet dish if you call by Friday.

5 _____

6 _____

7 _____

8 _____

Name _____

The Animal Chorus

Find the naming part that fits each sentence.
Then write each naming part in the correct
place in the puzzle.

Geese	Dogs
Pigs	Sheep
Cats	Horses
Frogs	Cows

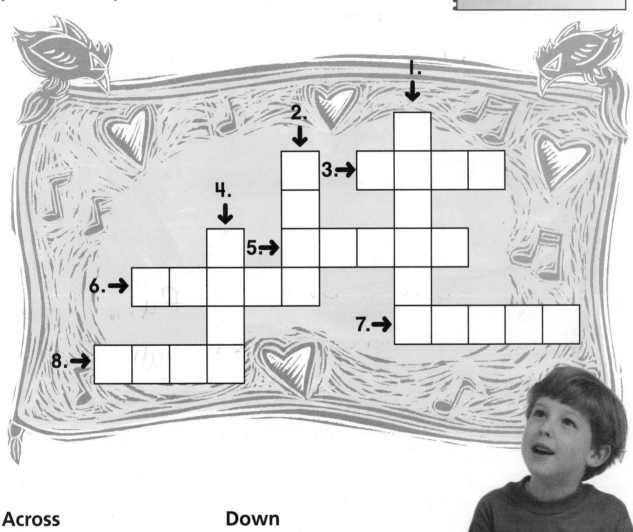

Across

3. ____ moo.

5. ____ honk.

6. ____ hop.

7. ____ bleat.

8. ____ meow.

Down

1. ____ gallop.

2. ____ grunt.

4. ____ bark.

Name John Thomas

Map It Out!

Draw or write about what happens in your story.

Beginning What happens first?

> I like my bog.
> Went I play
> baskitball.

Middle What happens next?

> Baskitball is fun.
> I love baskitball.

End What happens last?

> I love Football.
> Football is fun.

Name _John Thomas_

Check It Out!

> ## • Revising Checklist •
>
> Answer these questions about your story.
>
> ☐ Do I tell what my characters look like?
> ☐ Do I tell what my characters say?
> ☐ Does my story have a beginning?
> ☐ Does the middle of my story tell what happens?
> ☐ Does my story have a good ending?

Write some titles for your story. Circle the one you like best.

_____

_____

_____

_____

Questions to Ask My Writing Partner

- Does my title make you want to read more?
- What do you like best about my story?
- Can you picture my characters?
- Do I need to tell more?

Name

A Special Pet

teach	taught
sharing	special
learned	

Laura wrote about her new pet in a journal.
Read what she wrote and finish the sentences.

Monday   In just one hour, my new pet will come home. First,

I will pick a _____ name for him.

Tuesday   I named my pet Buddy because he is my friend.

Today I will _____ Buddy a trick.

Wednesday   Yesterday I _____ Buddy to sit

and stay. I gave him a treat for being good.

Thursday   I _____ to give Buddy a bath.

Friday   I told my friends to come and play. I like

_____ Buddy with them.

Playing together is better than playing alone.

What kind of pet do
you think Buddy is?
Draw a picture.

Name John Thomas

A Letter to Granddaddy

Help Maya write a letter to her granddaddy.
She wants to tell him all about Julius.

Dear Granddaddy,

Julius has been here for two months. We love to

hug him_____.

He loves to eat cakejes_____

_____. We go to stores and

_____.

There are some problems with Julius. Mom and

Dad say he is too _____. He is

too noisy when he _____

_____. That is why I am trying

to teach him _____. Then Mom

and Dad will love him as much as I do!

Love,

Maya

Pet Show Today! 31

Can a Pig Do That?

Use green to color the things a real pig can do. Use
red to color the things that only a fantasy pig can do.

1 take naps

2 get a job

3 tell a joke

4 win a singing contest

5 live in a barn

6 eat corn

7 drive a truck

8 roll in mud

Finish these sentences about pigs.

A real pig can _____

_____

A fantasy pig can _____

_____

Name

A Pig for a Pet?

Write a word from the box to finish each sentence.
Cut out each sentence and paste it to the pig with
the same beginning sound as the word you wrote.

Read with a partner what the pigs say.

1 Do you _____ a pig
would make a good pet?

3 _____ would
the pig live?

2 It could stay in
_____ old shed.

4 _____ do you like
pigs so much?

 Pet Show Today! **33**

Pet Show Rhymes

Complete the rhymes. Cut out and paste each animal's picture next to the ribbon it won.

better	hour	pick
stay	told	

1 This pet can _____ up fish.

And eat them from a dish.

2 The second prize pet is sure to roar,

If he must _____ for an

_____ or more.

3 Long ears and big feet win prize three!

A _____ pet you will not see.

4 Just look at this pet's bulging eyes.

They _____ me that he won

fourth prize.

Name

The ABC Pet Show

Let's get the pet show in order. Read the words in each box. Write the three words in ABC order.

1 _____

wait
stop
go

_____

_____

2 _____

up
in
out

_____

_____

3 _____

pig
cat
dog

_____

_____

Write the names of three pets in ABC order. Draw a picture of each pet.

4 _____   _____   _____

Pet Show Today!   37

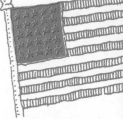

Name _____

A Pig in the Classroom

What if Julius came to your school? Finish these sentences.

1 One day, _____ came to my school.

2 My teacher _____.

Now write three sentences that tell what Julius

did in your classroom. Then draw Julius in the picture.

3 _____

4 _____

5 _____

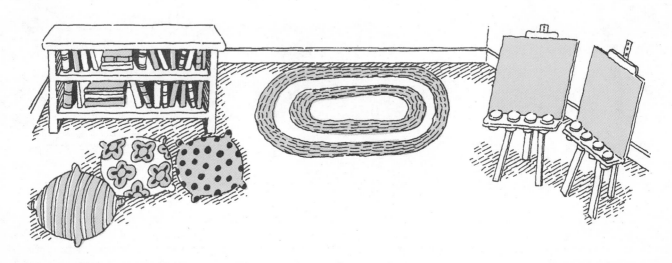

Name

Perfect Pigs

Each Spelling Word is spelled with **th** or **wh**. The letters **th** spell two different sounds in these words. The letters **wh** spell one sound.

Spelling Words	
1. **that**	5. **than**
2. **them**	6. **white**
3. **when**	7. **thin**
4. **with**	8. **which**

 Your Own Words

the th sounds → that
→ thin

the wh sound → when

Complete each puzzle. Write the Spelling Words that have the spelling shown on the snout of each pig. Then color the squares that have the letters **th** or **wh**.

Write Spelling Words to answer the questions.

1 Which word ends with the last sound you hear in **dream**? _____

2 Which word rhymes with **hen**? _____

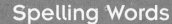

Spelling Spree

Write the missing Spelling Words.

Spelling Words	
1. **that**	5. **than**
2. **them**	6. **white**
3. **when**	7. **thin**
4. **with**	8. **which**

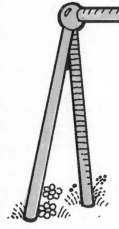

1. **thick** or _____

2. **black** and _____

3. **where** or _____

4. **this** or _____

Find and circle four Spelling Words that are spelled wrong in this post card. Then write each word correctly.

Dear Wendy,

    I hope you are having fun whith the pig. He dances better thann I do. I am glad you got the hats. Please tell me wich one Jingles ate. I will send you a new one. Tell your mom and dad that I love tem.

          Love,

          Uncle Pete

5. _____

6. _____

7. _____

8. _____

Color Me Pink

Color pink the puzzle pieces with action parts.

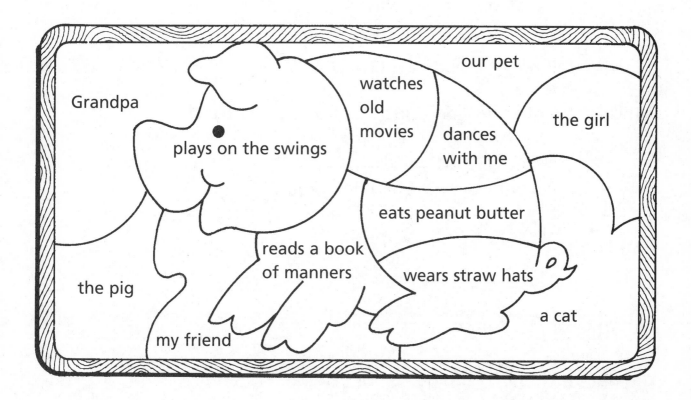

Grandpa

plays on the swings

watches
old
movies

our pet

dances
with me

the girl

eats peanut butter

reads a book
of manners

wears straw hats

the pig

my friend

a cat

Write the action parts to finish these sentences.

Example: The pig <u>eats peanut butter.</u>

1 Our pet _____.

2 The girl _____.

3 A cat _____.

4 Grandpa _____.

5 My friend _____.

Name

The Award Goes To . . .

Pick a character from Pet Show Today! who
has a pet. Make an award that tells why he
or she is a great pet owner. Answer the
questions to help you get started.

Which pet owner do you think should get an award?

_____

Why does this pet owner deserve an award?

1 _____

2 _____

3 _____

The award should tell why the pet owner is good at taking
care of a pet. Present your award to the class or group. Tell
whether the pet owner and the pet are realistic or fantasy.

Checklist

Before you present the award, use this
checklist to check your work.

☐ My award tells about a great pet owner.

☐ My award tells why this pet owner should win.

☐ I can explain what is real or not real about the
pet owner and the pet.

Name _____

Lights, Camera, Action!

Plan a movie about an animal in **Animal Tracks**.

Which animal will you choose?

Topic

What is one important idea about your animal?

Main Idea

What details do you want to tell about your animal?

Supporting Details

On the next page, show what your movie will look like. ➡

Be a Nature Detective 43

**Make a story board of your movie. Draw pictures and
write sentences to tell the story.**

Tell your movie idea to a partner.

Be a Nature Detective

Animal Rhymes

Read the beginnings of the rhymes. Cut out and
paste the words that complete the rhymes.

1 A turtle really can't move _____ .

So in a race, it comes in _____ .

2 Rabbits move quite fast, I _____ .

They hop away in just a _____ .

3 Behind the tree, I saw a _____ .

It tried to hide behind the _____ .

4 A raccoon got into our _____ .

Before too long, we heard a _____ .

| trash |
| wink |
| trunk |
| last |
| crash |
| fast |
| skunk |
| think |

On the next page, write an animal rhyme. ➡

Be a Nature Detective **45**

Write an animal rhyme of your own.

_____

_____

_____

_____

_____

_____

_____

_____

Name

Track Down the Right Word

The park ranger can help you enjoy a walk.
Write the words to finish her speech.

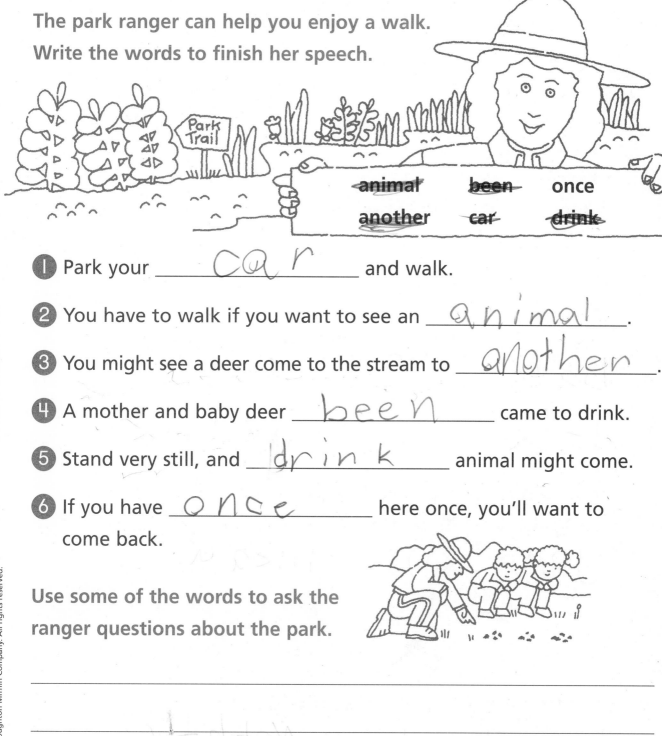

| animal | been | once |
| another | car | drink |

1 Park your ___car___ and walk.

2 You have to walk if you want to see an ___animal___.

3 You might see a deer come to the stream to ___another___.

4 A mother and baby deer ___been___ came to drink.

5 Stand very still, and ___drink___ animal might come.

6 If you have ___once___ here once, you'll want to
come back.

Use some of the words to ask the
ranger questions about the park.

_____

_____

_____

Name ....

What Do You Mean?

Read the two meanings for each word. Then
write a sentence for each meaning.

Example:

fly

A **fly** is a kind of insect.

To **fly** is to travel through the air.

A fly buzzed around my nose.

Birds fly from tree to tree.

bat

A **bat** is a thick stick used to hit a ball.

A **bat** is a small animal with wings and a body like a mouse.

1 <u>bats naugs on clats</u>

2 _____

mean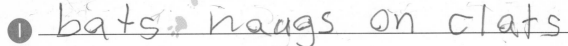

To **mean** is to say the same thing as.

To be **mean** is to not be friendly or kind.

3 <u>you are mean.</u>

4 _____

watch

To **watch** means to look at something to see what it will do.

A **watch** is a small clock you wear on your wrist.

5 <u>I like to watch t.k</u>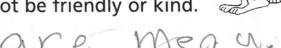

6 _____

Question and Answer

Look at the picture. Then write a sentence to answer each question. Remember to write complete sentences.

1 What is the mother bird doing?

To get food.

2 Which animal is swimming in the river?

Duck trdol

3 What is the rabbit doing?

hoping

4 Which animal is washing its hands?

rakon

Now make up your own question about an animal in the picture. Trade papers with a friend. Answer each other's questions.

Question: _____

Answer: _____

Name

Sound Tracks

Each Spelling Word has the short **a**, short **i**, or short **u** vowel sound. The short **a** sound may be spelled **a**. The short **i** sound may be spelled **i**. The short **u** sound may be spelled **u**.

	Spelling Words	
1. **mud**	5. **jump**
2. **is**	6. **fast**
3. **ran**	7. **cut**
4. **has**	8. **fish**

 Your Own Words

the short a sound → ran

the short i sound → is

the short u sound → mud

Write each Spelling Word on the animal whose name has the same short vowel sound.

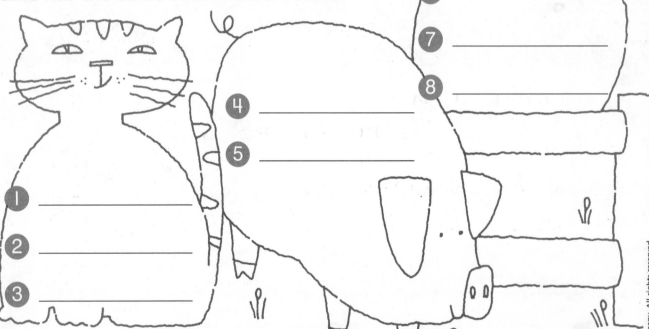

6 _____

7 _____

8 _____

4 _____

5 _____

1 _____

2 _____

3 _____

Write Spelling Words to answer the questions.

9 Which word ends with the **sh** sound? _____

10 Which word rhymes with **past**? _____

Spelling Spree

Write a Spelling Word to finish the second sentence in each pair.

Spelling Words	
1. **mud**	5. **jump**
2. **is**	6. **fast**
3. **ran**	7. **cut**
4. **has**	8. **fish**

1. The opposite of **first** is **last**.
   The opposite of **slow** is _____.

2. You can **chop** a piece of **wood**.
   You can _____ a piece of **paper**.

3. A person has **legs**.
   A _____ has **fins**.

4. **Lions** cool off in the **shade**.
   Pigs cool off in the _____.

1 _____

2 _____

3 _____

4 _____

Find and circle four Spelling Words that are spelled wrong in this log. Write each word correctly.

My Science Log

The sun iz coming up. We see raccoon tracks in the snow. Each footprint hass four long toes. The raccoon rann along the river. We will have to move fast to catch up with it. First, we have to jemp over a stone wall.

5 _____

6 _____

7 _____

8 _____

Name

Who's Been Here?

Unscramble the words in each
box. Write each sentence correctly.

twigs used from they trees

3 _____

_____

this made who dam

1 _____

_____

made it beavers some

2 _____

_____

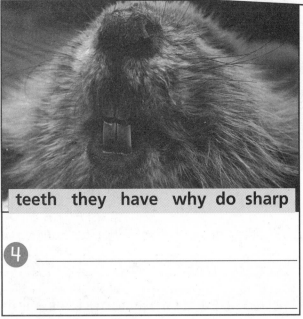

teeth they have why do sharp

4 _____

_____

Write a telling sentence about one of the pictures.

5 _____

Write a question about one of the pictures.

6 _____

Nature Clues

Write the words in the puzzle to fit the clues.

curious	bird
spy	eye
discover	notice
small	size
green	close

Across

1. Can you hear a _____ chirping?
7. When you wink, you close one _____.
8. When you are busy, you might not _____ something.
9. Things look different when you take a _____ look.
10. If you watch an animal quietly, you can be a nature _____!

Down

2. If you look around, you will _____ new things.
3. To know if something will fit, it helps to know its _____.
4. If you want to know about something, you are _____.
5. The color of many leaves is _____.
6. Another word for **little** is _____.

Name

Look Closely

Complete the chart.

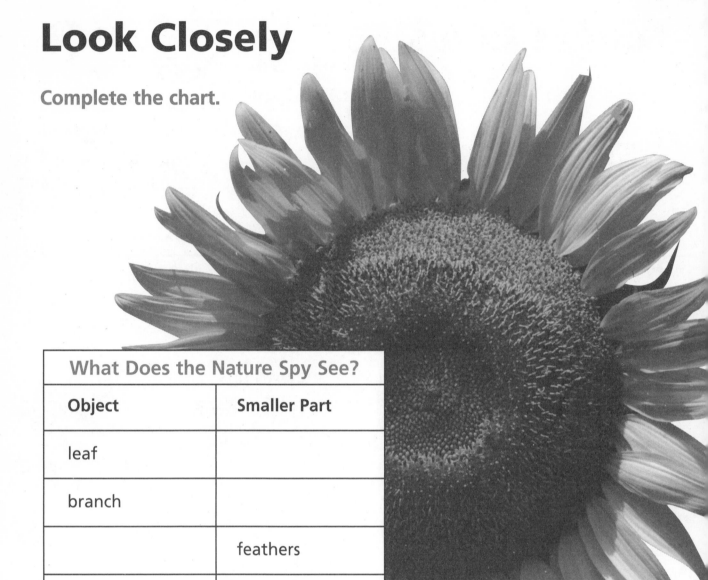

What Does the Nature Spy See?	
Object	**Smaller Part**
leaf	
branch	
	feathers
	golden eye
sunflower	
ice	

Why does the girl's mother call her a nature spy?

_____

_____

Turtles and Frogs

**Read more about two animals you saw in Nature Spy. Then
fill in the chart to tell how they are alike and different.**

Turtles are cold-blooded animals. They sit in the sun to
warm up. They move to the shade or water to get cool. Most
turtles live both on land and in water. On land they move very slowly.
To keep safe from other animals, turtles pull their heads, feet, and tails
into their hard shells.

Frogs are cold-blooded, too. The sun warms them up when they feel cold.
Like turtles, most frogs live on land and in water. But frogs move
very quickly. They use their speed to keep safe from other animals.

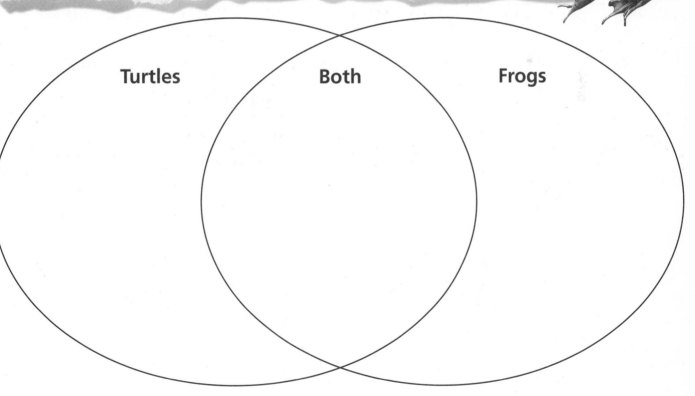

Turtles   Both   Frogs

**Work with a partner to find out more about turtles and frogs.
Add what you learn to the chart.**

Be a Nature Detective 55

Name

Can You Imagine!

Would a nature spy ever see these silly things? Write a
word to complete each sentence so it tells about the picture.

1 There's a bird wearing a _____. (nest, vest)

2 The bee is tired and is taking a _____. (rest, test)

3 The little toad is all ready to _____. (chop, shop)

4 There's a spider learning to _____. (hop, drop)

5 Some ants don't want to get _____. (net, wet)

6 Look! The fish has a worm for a _____. (set, pet)

On the line below,
write a silly sentence
of your own about an
animal. Draw a
picture of your animal.

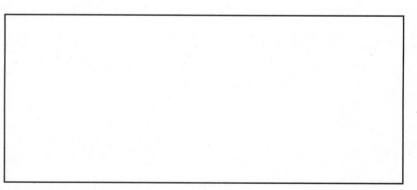

7 _____

Nature Notes

Pretend you're a nature spy. Write a word from the box to complete each sentence.

| small | size | eye | close | bird |

I think I discovered a new animal!

1 It had the body of a mouse, but the feet of a _____.

2 It was _____, so I wasn't afraid.

3 I took a _____ look.

4 I saw it had just one bright green _____.

5 The large _____ of its ears surprised me.

The animal made a funny noise. It mooed like a cow!

Draw a picture of the animal. Write its name.

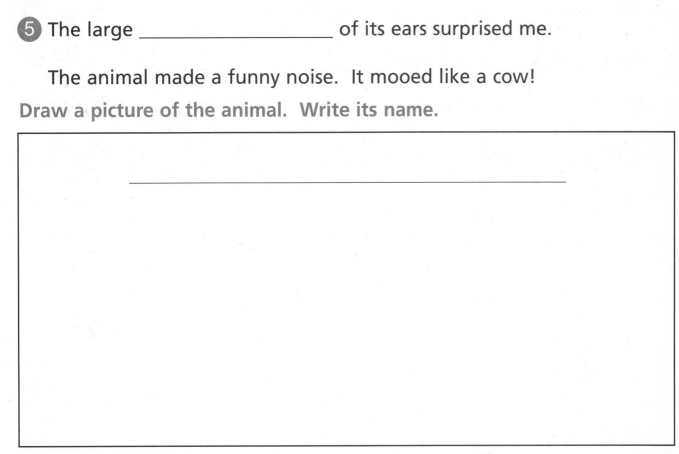

_____

Name

ABC Spy

There's always something to see when you're a nature spy. Write the words in ABC order.

bird
bug
bark

1. _____
   _____
   _____

frog
feathers
flower

2. _____
   _____
   _____

look
leaf
lines

3. _____
   _____
   _____

sunflower
seed
spider

4. _____
   _____
   _____

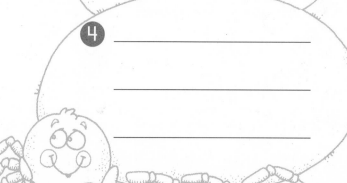

What Do You See?

Use the words in the box to write sentences about what you see. First, write a question. Next, write two telling sentences. Then write an exclamation.

ant
anthill
food
strong

1 **Question:** _____

_____

2 **Telling Sentence:** _____

_____

3 **Telling Sentence:** _____

_____

4 **Exclamation:** _____

_____

Do your sentences all begin with a capital letter?
Do they end with the right end mark?

Be a Nature Detective **59**

Changing Colors

Spelling Words

1. **web**   5. **spot**
2. **rock** 6. **leg**
3. **nest** 7. **pet**
4. **pod**   8. **job**

Your Own Words

Each Spelling Word has the short **e** or the short **o** vowel sound. The short **e** sound may be spelled **e**. The short **o** sound may be spelled **o**.

 the short e sound ➜ web

the short o sound ➜ rock

Write the Spelling Words on the leaves. Color yellow the leaves with the words that have the first sound you hear in 🐘. Color orange the leaves with the words that have the first sound you hear in 🦩.

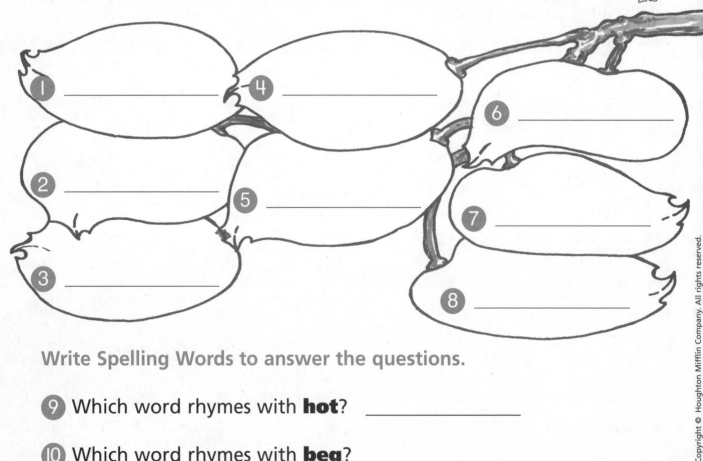

1. _____
2. _____
3. _____
4. _____
5. _____
6. _____
7. _____
8. _____

Write Spelling Words to answer the questions.

9 Which word rhymes with **hot**? _____

10 Which word rhymes with **beg**? _____

Name

Spelling Spree

Write a Spelling Word for each clue.

Spelling Words	
1. web	5. spot
2. rock	6. leg
3. nest	7. pet
4. pod	8. job

1. It rhymes with **clock**. It begins like **race**.

2. It rhymes with **best**. It begins like **nut**.

3. It rhymes with **let**. It begins like **party**.

4. It rhymes with **rod**. It begins like **person**.

① _____   ③ _____

② _____   ④ _____

Find and circle four Spelling Words that are wrong in this book review. Then write each word correctly.

The pictures in this nature book are the best! The author did a fine jawb of showing many kinds of plants and animals. You will see a spider spinning a webb and a robin making a nest. Look closely and you can spat the lines on a leaf and the seeds in a pod. There is even a close-up picture of a frog's leag.

⑤ _____

⑥ _____

⑦ _____

⑧ _____

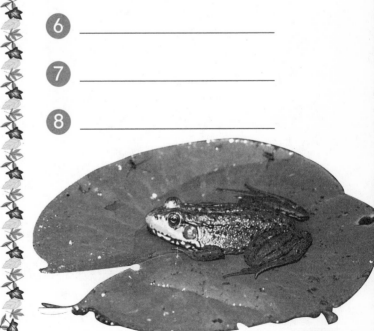

Name _____

Spinning Sentences

A spider has made a word web. Use words that are joined together to write two telling sentences, two questions, and two exclamations.

Example: They can jump so far!

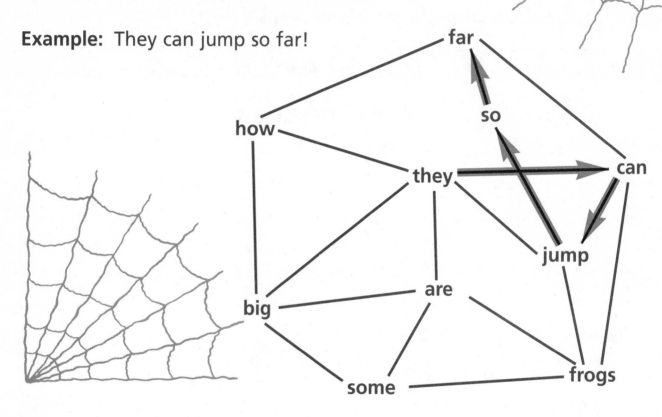

1 _____

2 _____

3 _____

4 _____

5 _____

6 _____

Step by Step

What will your instructions tell how to do?

_____

Write your ideas for your instructions in the chart.

Materials
What does someone need to do this?
Steps
What are the steps for your instructions?   **Write them in order and number them.**

Take Another Look

• Revising Checklist •

Use these questions to think about your writing.

Are the steps for my instructions in the right

order? _____

What time-order words did I use?

_____

What can I change or add to make my instructions better?

_____

_____

_____

_____

Questions to Ask

My Writing Partner

• Are my instructions clear?

• Are my steps in an order
  that makes sense?

• Do I need to add
  anything to my
  instructions?

Name

Great News!

Write words from the box to
complete this ad.

grow	open
smooth	outgrow
enemies	opening
goes	hollow

Suzy's Seashells — Biggest Sale Ever!

What does this mean?

It means most of our shells are half price.

Cone Shells Only 50¢ Each!

These shells are as _____ as glass.

Chambered Nautilus $5.95!

These are cut in half so you can see they are _____.

Live Hermit Crabs Only $2.95!

See the hermit crab hide from its _____.

It goes into an old shell and covers the _____.

Feed Our Sea Turtles!

Watch them _____.

(When they _____ the tank,

each turtle _____ back to the sea.)

The store is _____ every day.

Name

In a Shell

Think about **What Lives in a Shell?**

Then write about the animal in the photo.

snail

_____

_____

_____

turtle

_____

_____

_____

hermit crab

_____

Draw and label other animals with shells.

_____   _____

Name

Which Is It?

Is each animal pictured at the bottom of the page a mollusk or a crustacean? Read the definitions. Then cut out and paste each animal in the correct column.

Mollusk	**Crustacean**
It has a soft mushy body. It usually lives inside a hard shell.	It lives in or near the water. It has legs and a shell that fits like armor.

shrimp

lobster

scallop

mussel

nautilus

spider crab

Name

Home Sweet Home

Read the sentences. Draw a circle around each word that has a long vowel sound and the CVC**e** pattern.

1 A turtle's shell is its home.

2 A bear likes to sleep in a cave.

3 A snail's shell keeps it safe.

4 A nest is a nice place for a bird.

5 Clams can open and close their shells.

Now write each word you circled in the shell that has the same vowel sound and the CVC**e** pattern. Add words of your own in each shell.

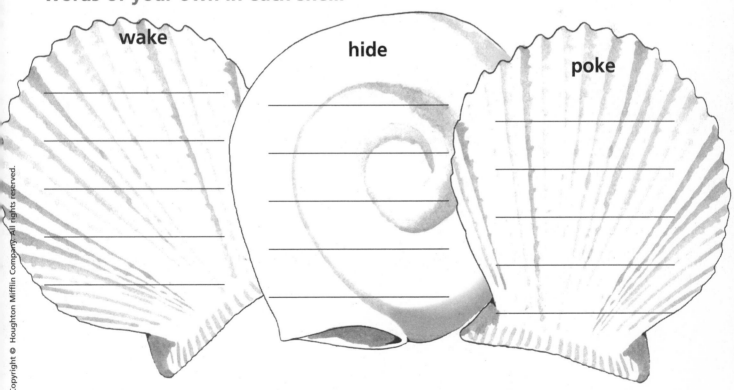

wake

_____

_____

_____

_____

hide

_____

_____

_____

_____

poke

_____

_____

_____

_____

Ex-shell-ent!

Read the recipe. Write an answer to each question.

Shellfish Stew

What you need:

4 cloves of garlic

1 tablespoon of oil

1 large can of tomatoes

juice of a lemon

4 cups of fish broth

1 pound each of scallops, clams, and shrimp

1 What goes into the stew?

_____

_____

2 What do you open with a can opener?

_____

3 Which thing can grow on a tree?

_____

4 What kinds of shellfish does the recipe say to use?

_____

5 What kind of shellfish do you like most?

_____

Name

Match the Opposites

Cut out and paste each word next to its opposite.

1   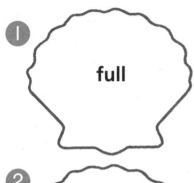 full

4    happy

2    pretty

5    interesting

3   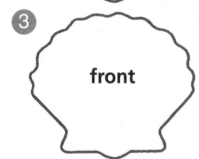 front

6    wet

On the back of this page, write two sentences using one of the word pairs.   ➡

sad	back	dry
boring	empty	ugly

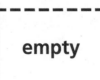

Write two sentences using one of the word pairs.

_____

_____

_____

_____

Name _____

What Will I Say?

Write the main idea for your paragraph in the middle circle. Think of examples or details that tell about your main idea. Write them in the other circles.

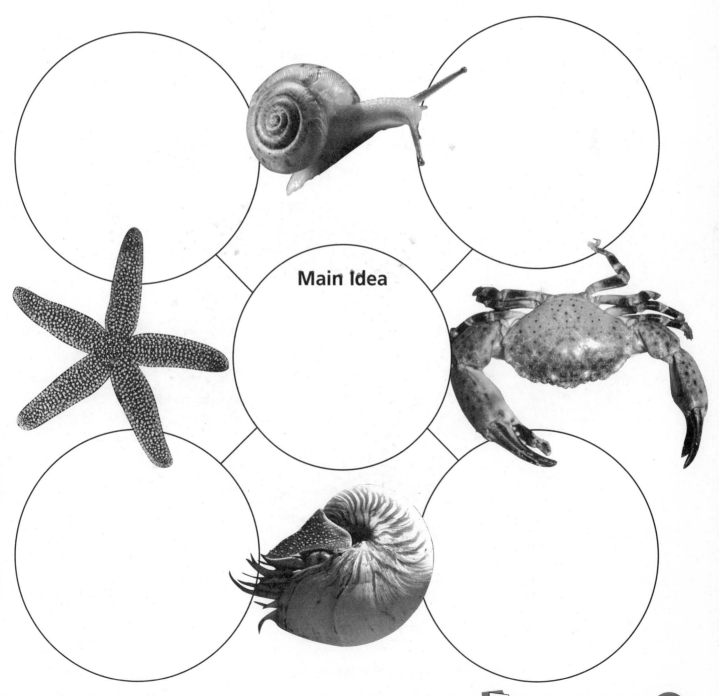

Main Idea

Name _____

By the Seashore

Each Spelling Word has a long vowel sound.
A long vowel sound may be spelled by the
vowel-consonant-**e** pattern.

long a → game   long o → home

long e → these   long u → use

long i → like

Spelling Words

1. **home**   5. **close**
2. **game**   6. **like**
3. **made**   7. **size**
4. **use**   8. **these**

Your Own Words

Write each Spelling Word on the box that has the matching long vowel sound.

1 _____

2 _____

4 _____

5 _____

3 _____

6 _____

7 _____

8 _____

Write Spelling Words to answer the questions.

9 Which word begins like **clam**? _____

10 Which word begins with the **th** sound? _____

Spelling Spree

Write a Spelling Word for each clue.
Then use the letters in the boxes to find
out where a snail lives.

1 how big something is ⬜ ___ ___ ___

2 this, that, _____ , those ___ ⬜ ___ ___ ___ ___

3 you play this for fun ___ ___ ___ ⬜

4 to shut ___ ⬜ ___ ___ ___

5 the same ⬜ ___ ___ ___

Secret Word: ___ ___ ___ ___ ___

Find and circle three Spelling Words that are spelled wrong
in this report. Then write each word correctly.

All About Snails

A land snail maide this shell. The shell is the
snail's hom. It keeps the snail safe. It is just the
right size to hold its body.

A land snail has one big foot. It can uze its
foot to move. Most land snails have lungs, like us.

6 _____

7 _____

8 _____

Name

Snail Shell

Color yellow the puzzle parts that have sentences.

Write each sentence correctly.

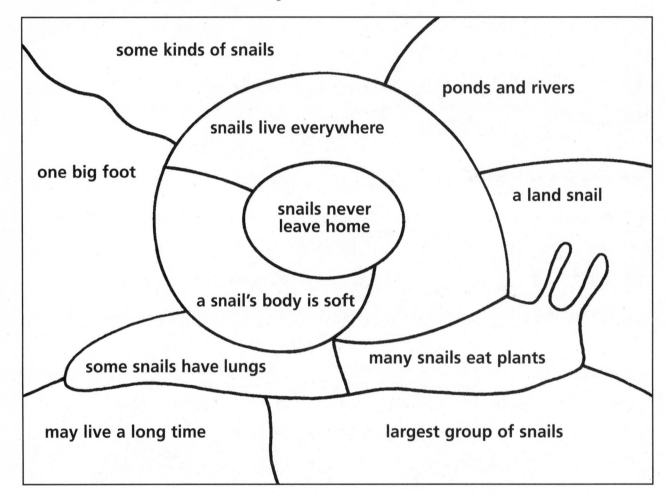

some kinds of snails

ponds and rivers

snails live everywhere

one big foot

a land snail

snails never
leave home

a snail's body is soft

some snails have lungs

many snails eat plants

may live a long time

largest group of snails

1 _____

2 _____

3 _____

4 _____

5 _____

Treasure Hunt

Little Treasure Island

This note can lead you to the treasure
on the island. Make each mark on the map.

1. Look for the shell at the edge of the sea. Put an **X** on it.

2. Walk past two tide-pools. Circle them.

3. Then follow footprints in the sand till you get to the dunes. Draw a brown flag on top of the dunes.

4. Climb down from the dunes and find the train tracks. Put a **T** on the tracks.

5. Look for something that has a sweet smell in one of the hollows in the ground. Put an **S** on it.

6. Now find something that can help you see better at twilight. Draw a box around it. The treasure is right underneath!

Name _____

Did That Really Happen?

Read each sentence about **Where Does the Trail Lead?**

Is it true or not true? Circle what you think.

1 The story takes place on an island in the winter. True Not True

_____

2 A boy walks all around and explores the island. True Not True

_____

3 The island is completely flat. True Not True

_____

4 Everything on the island is close to the edge of the sea. True Not True

_____

5 There are birds, but no other animals, on the island. True Not True

_____

6 Some things on the island are old and not used any more. True Not True

_____

7 At the end of the day, the boy is back where he started, at the edge of the sea. True Not True

_____

Look at the sentences that are not true.

Rewrite each one to make it true.

78 **Be a Nature Detective**

Look for Clues

Someone or something is in an old shanty. Read the report.

Report by Officer Shelstein of the Beach Patrol

    I passed by a shanty by the sea. I heard a pecking noise. I peeked in the window. I didn't see anything. I decided to go inside. There were feathers everywhere. There were also bits of berries and pieces of dry bread. As I walked around, I thought I heard a flapping sound. The sound scared me. Then I smelled something. Something fishy was going on here! Sure enough, there were some half-eaten fish near the window. I had seen, heard, and smelled enough. I knew what was living in the shanty.

Who or what is inside?

_____

Write the details that helped you decide.

_____

_____

_____

_____

Name

Summertime Island Message

Underline the compound words in the post card. Then write sentences to finish the message. Use the words in the box to make compound words.

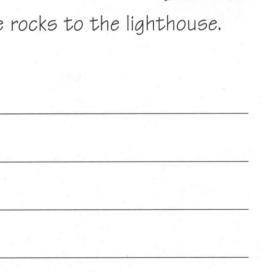

| boat | night | fire | sail | time | camp |

Summertime Island

Hi, everybody!

How do you like my summer island?

Wherever you go on the island there is something to do.

Sometimes I race my friends across the rocks to the lighthouse.

Other times I go sailing.

_____

_____

_____

_____

Name

Beach Party

Circle the words that end with the sounds you hear at the end of **band**, **wing**, or **sink**. Then draw a line to connect the words you circled. Where does the trail lead? Circle the picture.

START

bring

neck

hand

wig

sad

book

big

thank

said

swing

hang

pin

hook

sick

hug

wind

chunk

land

Use some of the words you circled to write a sentence about the beach.

_____

_____

Be a Nature Detective **81**

Name

Do You Know Me?

| smell | brown | sea |
| lead | island | |

Write the words to answer the riddles.

1
I can be big.
I can be little.
I have water all around.
What am I?

_____

4
Is it a flower? Is it a fish?
Is it popcorn? Is it pie?
My nose can tell.
What am I?

_____

2
I've been called salty
And deep blue too.
Fish swim in me.
What am I?

_____

5
Don't follow.
Don't fall behind.
Do what my name says.
What word am I?

_____

3
Eyes can be blue.
Eyes can be green.
Eyes can be the color of me.
What color am I?

_____

6
Now try making up your
own riddle.

_____

_____

_____

_____

_____

Name

Trail Guide

Read each set of guide words. Cross out
the word that does not belong.

This book belongs to:

pen • pot
pin
pack
pine

pan • play
pose
pink
pet

fir • fox
flop
fun
foot

leg • low
like
load
late

shop • soft
sleep
small
same

bat • bow
bet
build
big

car • cold
city
cube
cent

wave • wind
work
weak
why

Look up **trail** in your dictionary.

What guide words are on the page where you find **trail**?

_____

Write a sentence using the word **trail**.

_____

_____

Name

That's Exactly Right!

Write each
sentence. Replace
the underlined
words with more
exact nouns.

Example:

Our family stayed in a <u>place</u> at the seashore.
Our family stayed in a **cabin** at the seashore.

1 I liked to climb over <u>things</u> at the beach.

_____

2 There were many <u>plants</u> outside our house.

_____

3 <u>Birds</u> woke us up by making loud noises.

_____

4 We saw two <u>animals</u> along the trail.

_____

Write one more sentence about the picture.
Remember to use exact nouns.

5 _____

_____

Name _____

Sailboats in the Sea

Each Spelling Word ends with **nd**, **ng**, or **nk**.
In words that end with **nd**, you hear the
sounds of **n** and **d**. In words that end with
ng or **nk**, you may not hear the sound of **n**.

nd → sa**nd**
ng → thi**ng**
nk → si**nk**

<table>
<tr><td colspan="2">**Spelling Words**</td></tr>
<tr><td>1. **sand**</td><td>5. **honk**</td></tr>
<tr><td>2. **sink**</td><td>6. **thing**</td></tr>
<tr><td>3. **and**</td><td>7. **thank**</td></tr>
<tr><td>4. **wind**</td><td>8. **sing**</td></tr>
<tr><td colspan="2">✎ Your Own Words</td></tr>
</table>

Complete each puzzle. Write each Spelling
Word on the sailboat that has the matching
spelling for the **nd**, **ng**, and **nk** sounds.

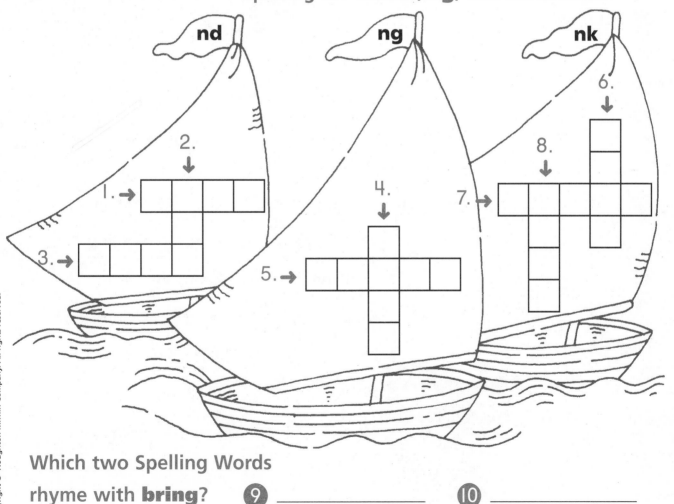

Which two Spelling Words
rhyme with **bring**?   ⑨ _____   ⑩ _____

Name _____

Spelling Spree

Spelling Words

1. **sand**	5. **honk**
2. **sink**	6. **thing**
3. **and**	7. **thank**
4. **wind**	8. **sing**

Think how the words in each group are alike.
Write the missing Spelling Words.

1 clay, dirt, _____

2 quack, cluck, _____

3 clouds, rain, _____

4 hum, whistle, _____

Find and circle four Spelling Words that are wrong in this
thank-you note. Then write each word correctly.

5 _____

6 _____

7 _____

8 _____

Dear Aunt Minna,

I want to thanc you for letting us stay in

your house by the sea. Every evening we

watched the sun cink into the ocean. Then

Mom, Dad, andd I would take a long walk

along the beach. The sand felt cool under

our feet. But the thig I liked best was when

we would sing songs by the campfire.

Love,

Spencer

Name

Don't Get Lost!

Help the boy find his way back to his family.
He can follow only the trails that have
nouns on them.

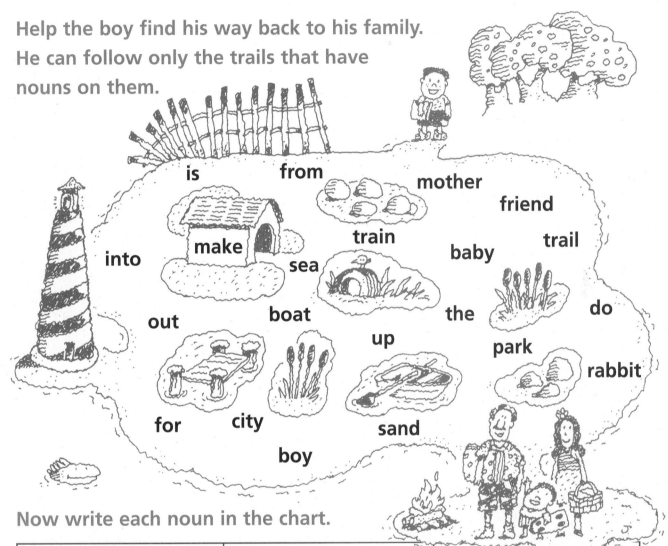

is from mother friend

into make train trail

sea baby

out boat the do

up park

for city sand rabbit

boy

Now write each noun in the chart.

People	Places	Things

Name

Making Nature Detective Pictures

Animals live all around us.
But they often hide from us.
Can you tell what animal is
hiding behind the rock?

Write two animals that live in each place.

Tell where each animal might hide.

In a Forest	Near a Pond

On another sheet of paper, draw forest and pond pictures.
Draw the animals in their hiding places. Make sure part of
each animal shows as a clue. Draw another clue for each
animal too. Write the animal names below each picture.

Checklist

Use this list to check your work.

❏ I drew pictures of a forest and a pond.

❏ Each picture has two hiding animals.

❏ I drew a showing part and another clue for each animal.

❏ I wrote the animal names below each picture.

What Is the Point?

Read this diary entry about the first day of school.
Then answer the questions.

Dear Diary,

What a day! I started second grade today.
I didn't know my classmates. And they didn't
know me! I don't know how to make friends.
Maybe the teacher has some ideas. In fact, today
he had us share things about ourselves. I didn't
know what to say, so I said that I play soccer. I'm
glad the first day of school is over. It was tough.

Author's Viewpoint
How did this writer feel about the first day of school?

Details
How do you know?

On another sheet of paper, write what the first day of school
was like for you.

Name

Train Ride!

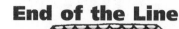

End of the Line

Play this game with a friend.
Make six cards with **day** on them
and make six cards with **train**.

Start: Each player places a marker
on the **Train Station**. Mix
the cards.

1. Take a card.
2. Move your marker to the word with
   a long **a** sound that has the same
   spelling as the word on the card.
3. Read the word and use it in a
   sentence.
4. If you can't read the word, go back
   one space.
5. Your turn is over. The next player
   gets a turn.

The first one to get to the **End of
the Line** wins.

Train Station

sand
main
tray
braid
may
lap
stray

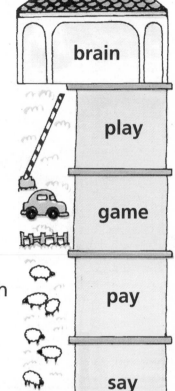

brain
play
game
pay
say
gate
grain
stay

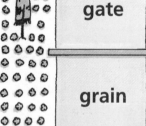

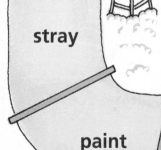

| paint | tame | gray | chain | map |

Name

A Reply to a Friend

Read this letter from one friend to another.

Dear Ricky,

How do you like your new school? Have you found many boys and <u>girls</u> to play with yet?

When you moved away <u>last</u> summer, I <u>didn't</u> have anyone to play with for a while. And you know I don't like to play by <u>myself</u>.

Did you know I am <u>flying</u> up to see you next year? Please write me <u>soon</u> and let me know how you are.

Your friend,

Terry

Write an answer. Use some of the underlined words.

Dear Terry,

_____

_____

_____

_____

_____

_____

Your friend,

Ricky

Name _____

Word Family Trees

Find the word families for **care**, **farm**, and **bake**, and write them on the family trees. Then make your own word family tree.

cares   farming

farmer

careful

bakery

c	a	r	e

b	a	k	e

f	a	r	m

_____

_____

_____

_____

baker   farmed

careless   baked

Keep in Touch!

Write your address in the first box. Then write the
addresses of two of your friends.

My Address

_____

_____

_____

My Friend's Address

_____

_____

_____

My Friend's Address

_____

_____

_____

Hooray for A!

Each Spelling Word has the long **a** vowel sound. This vowel sound may be spelled **ay** or **ai**.

the long a sound ➜ play, train

Write each Spelling Word on the easel that has the matching spelling for the long a sound.

ai

1. _____
2. _____
3. _____
4. _____

ay

5. _____
6. _____
7. _____
8. _____

Which two Spelling Words begin with consonant clusters?

9 _____   10 _____

Name _____

Spelling Spree

Write a Spelling Word to finish each sign.
Begin each word with a capital letter.

Spelling Words	
1. **train**	5. **way**
2. **play**	6. **rain**
3. **day**	7. **sail**
4. **paint**	8. **pay**

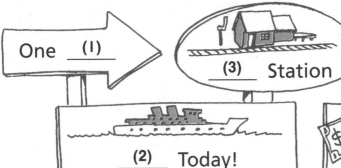

One ___(1)___

___(3)___ Station

___(2)___ Today!

___(4)___ at the Door

1 _____

2 _____

3 _____

4 _____

Find and circle four Spelling Words that are spelled wrong
in this play. Then write each word correctly.

A New School in a New Land

Mom: This is a big daye for you, Suki. Do you want me to drive
you to school?

Suki: No, Mom, I know the way.

Mom: Take an umbrella. It is going to rayn.

Suki: I hope somebody will plai with me. When I get home,
I will paynt you a picture of my new school.

5 _____

6 _____

7 _____

8 _____

Special Friends

Write each sentence. Use the name of a special person, place, or thing in place of each picture clue.

special person **special place** **special thing**

1 I will visit my friend .

_____

2 Her house is on .

_____

3 The name of her school is .

_____

4 She has a sister named .

_____

5 Her cat is named .

_____

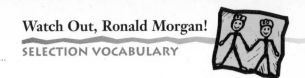

Name _____

Telephone Talk

Read what Ronald told his friend
James on the phone one night.
Write what James answered. Use
at least five words from the box.

best	frames	squint
blink	lenses	still
blue	round	
don't	sharp	

Ronald: Last week my teacher said that I may need glasses.
I do my best to read the words on the board, but the letters
aren't very sharp or clear anymore. What do you think?

James: _____

_____

Ronald: Sometimes I squint my eyes until they're nearly
shut and blink them until my lids hurt. But that still doesn't help.
Do you ever do that?

James: _____

_____

Ronald: Today, I took the lenses out of an old pair of blue
sunglasses and tried on the frames. The round frames don't look
too bad. In fact, they look good with my round head. Ha!

James: _____

_____

Name

Take a Good Look

Use what you know about **Watch Out, Ronald Morgan!** to complete this story map.

Characters:

Setting:

Problem:

Event:

Event:

Event:

Ending:

Use your story map to retell the story to a friend.

Name

Help!

The children in Miss Tyler's classroom are very helpful.

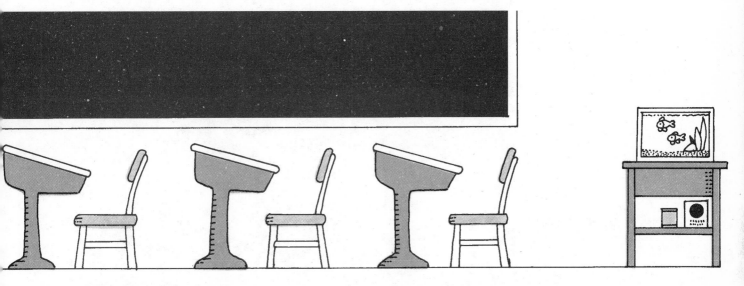

Cut out the four pictures of children. Paste the pictures
of helpful children in the classroom scene above. Write one
sentence that supports the generalization.

_____

_____

Name

Speak Before He Leaps!

Each pair of sentences warns Ronald about something.

Write a word with **ea** or **ee** to complete each sentence.

1 Stop! Don't _____ that to the gerbil.

feed   feet

Gerbils don't _____ candy.

read   eat

2 Wear a warm hat on your _____.

bread   head

You will _____ one on this cold day.

need   heat

3 Hey! There's a _____ in your cup.

squeak   leak

You'd better _____ up that mess.

clean   dream

Write a pair of sentences of your own to warn
Ronald about something. Use words with **ea** or **ee**.

_____

_____

_____

_____

Name

Let It Snow

Help Ronald Morgan make a snow person by using the words in the box to complete the directions. Then follow the directions and make a snow person.

| round |
| still |
| best |
| Don't |
| blue |

How to Make a Snow Person

1 Do your _____ to follow these directions.

2 Draw three circles, one on top of the other. The top one is the smallest, and the bottom one is the largest. Make the circles nice

and _____.

3 Draw a face on the smallest circle.

_____ forget to draw a nose.

4 You _____ aren't done. Add a hat.

5 Draw a striped scarf around the snow person's neck. Color the

stripes red and _____.

Words to Watch

Find three words in **Watch Out, Ronald Morgan!** that you do not understand. Look up each word in the dictionary and complete the dictionary entry.

Entry word: _____

Meaning: _____

_____

Entry word: _____

Meaning: _____

_____

Entry word: _____

Meaning: _____

_____

Make your own dictionary. Label a sheet of paper for each letter of the alphabet. Cut out the entries and paste them on the correct pages. Add words as you read more stories.

Name **John thomas   Nove 12, 2003**

Spelling Spree

1. **see**	5. **team**
2. **read**	6. **green**
3. **need**	7. **speak**
4. **please**	8. **feed**

Write the word that goes with each clue.

1 talk _____ **speak**

2 rhymes with **tree** _____ **team**

3 red, yellow, ____ _____ **see**

4 ____ and write _____ **green**

5 a baseball ____ _____ **feed**

Find and circle three Spelling Words
that are spelled wrong in these rules.
Write each word correctly.

School Rules

• Remember to fede the gerbil.

• Don't throw snowballs and
  pleaze don't slide on the ice.

• If you cannot read this, you
  nead glasses!

6 _____ **feed**

7 _____ **green**

8 _____ **see**

Name John Thomas

Time Out for Kickball

Ronald isn't sure which pronoun can take the place of each word or words. Help him by writing the correct pronoun on the other half of the kickball.

| he   she   it   they |

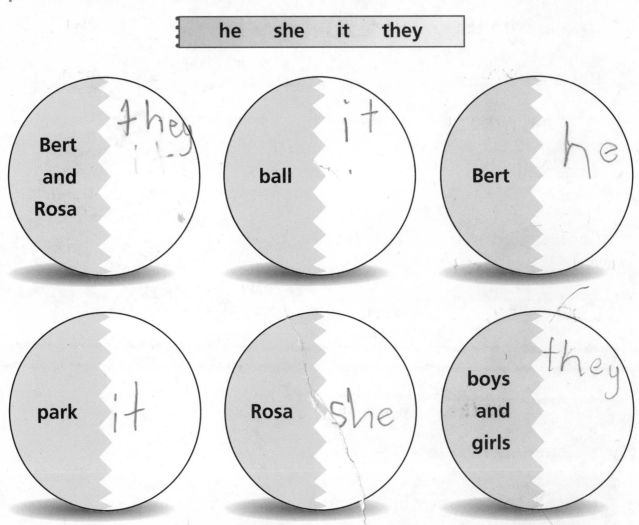

Bert and Rosa — they

ball — it

Bert — he

park — it

Rosa — she

boys and girls — they

Finish this story. Use at least two pronouns in your sentences.

Bert and Rosa played kickball after school. Me and Tevon plag evrey bay.

....

Name

Read This!

What is your favorite book? Write a book report about it. Remember to draw a line under the title.

The title is _____

The author is _____

This book is about _____

_____

_____

_____

_____

_____

I think this book _____

_____

_____

_____

_____

Name John Thomas Nove 12,2009

Keep Your Eyes Open

Each Spelling Word has the long **e** vowel sound.
This vowel sound may be spelled **ee** or **ea**.

the long e sound ➡ see, read

Connect the words with the long **e** sound to
reach Ronald's eyeglasses. Then write each
Spelling Word on the eye chart that has the
matching spelling for the long **e** sound.

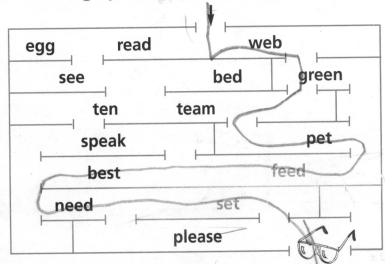

egg read web
see bed green
ten team
speak pet
best feed
need set
please

Write Spelling W____ nswer

the ____

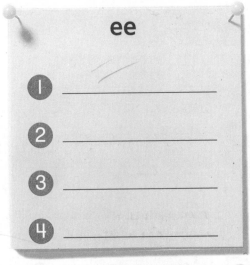

ee

1. _____
2. _____
3. _____
4. _____

ea

5. _____
6. _____
7. _____
8. _____

Name _____

Help Wanted

Read the want ad. Write the word to complete each sentence. Finish the sentence at the end.

wish	sneaked	crawled	boy	while
angry	through	heard	miss	

I've ___miss___ that great baby-sitters are out there.

We need one during summer vacation. My sister is one year old, and I am

an eight-year-old ___boy___.

You must be able to chase my sister. She has gotten into things ever

since she has ___crawled___. And you can't get

___angry___ when I play superheroes. The last baby-sitter

quit when I ___sneaked___ up on her and stormed

___through___ the house. We want to have fun

___through___ you are with us. Then we'll

___angry___ you when you leave. If you are a great

baby-sitter, I _____ you would call me.

P.S. Some things that my sister and I would like to do this summer are

_____

_____

Name _____Mutak_____

Baby-sitter Advice

Finish each sentence about What Kind of Baby-sitter Is This?

1 Kevin felt angry because

his muther was

leving.

_____

_____

2 Aunt Lovey came over to baby-sit. Kevin thought she would _be men._

_____

_____

3 Kevin saw Aunt Lovey

And he

thought she

would nice.

4 Kevin discovered that he and Aunt Lovey _that they_

would have fun.

He decided that _he would_

have fan.

How can you use what you learned from the story to be better friends with your own baby-sitter? Write your ideas.

_____

_____

_____

Name

Baby-sitters for Hire

**Read what the baby-sitters say. Which one would you
choose for a baby-sitter? Explain why.**

My name
is Roberta. I'm a sports nut.
On rainy days, we can watch sports on
TV. When it's nice, we can play in the
park. I don't like to cook, so we
can order pizza.

My name is Ana. I like
to put on plays and go on
long nature walks. I also make
terrific fudge brownies.

I like the frst baby siter
because She likes pizza and
I like pizza to.

Name

New Tricks for Old Words

Read each sentence. Follow the directions to change the underlined word to a different word with **oa** or **ow**.
Write the new word in the box. Then use it in a sentence.

1. Aunt Lovey saw an ad for <u>soap</u> on TV.
   Change the **s** to **c** and the **p** to **t** to make something to wear.

2. Kevin sat <u>down</u> with her, and they watched the ball game.
   Change the **d** to **t** and you have a place where people live.

3. They watched the star player <u>throw</u> a fastball to the batter.
   Take away the **th** and you have what someone does in a boat.

4. Kevin watched the ball <u>float</u> right past the batter.
   Change the **fl** to **g** and you have an animal that lives on a farm.

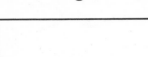

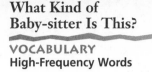

Mix and Match

Cut out the words at the bottom and paste them on the matching shapes. Then write your own words to finish the sentences.

Kevin's New Job

Today I'm taking care of a little boy. He was pretty good while I

was _____ with him. But then he started

_____ the house and up and

down the stairs.

Now he's _____. I think he might

_____. I she'd get back. Wait!

Was that a _____ I in the

_____? Hurray! She's back. Baby-sitting is

_____!

miss   heard   through   wish

Name

Take a Look Around

Use guide words to find each word in your dictionary. Write the guide words that are on the page with the word.

Word	Guide Words
baby-sitter	
bath	
school	
scratch	
porch	
pour	

For each set of guide words, write a word that you might find on that page. Use your dictionary for ideas.

Guide Words	Word
fold • fox	
woman • worth	
place • plum	
hand • have	

Name _____

Come One, Come All!

Imagine that your class is having a party. What kind of party will it be? Invite someone. Draw pictures on your invitation.

To _____

Please come to _____

_____

Date _____

Time _____

Place _____

_____

Given by _____

Go Team!

Each Spelling Word has the long **o** vowel
sound. The long **o** sound may be spelled
oa or **ow**.

the long o sound ➔ soap, own

Spelling Words

1. **own**	5. **bowl**
2. **soap**	6. **slow**
3. **coat**	7. **road**
4. **show**	8. **boat**

Your Own Words

Write the missing letters to make Spelling Words.
Then write the words under the pennants that have
the matching spelling for the long **o** sound.

s h ____ ____   r ____ ____ d   ____ ____ n

b ____ ____ l   c ____ ____ t   s ____ ____ p

s l ____ ____   b ____ ____ t

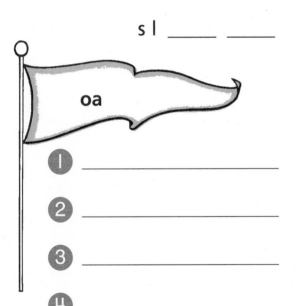

oa

1 _____
2 _____
3 _____
4 _____

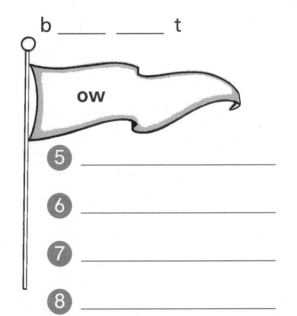

ow

5 _____
6 _____
7 _____
8 _____

Which two Spelling Words rhyme with **goat**?

9 _____   10 _____

Spelling Spree

Write the Spelling Word that answers the question and rhymes with the word in **dark print**.

Spelling Words	
1. **own**	5. **bowl**
2. **soap**	6. **slow**
3. **coat**	7. **road**
4. **show**	8. **boat**

1. What is a jacket for a bearded animal?

   a **goat** _____

2. What is a bird that does not fly fast?

   a _____ **crow**

3. What is a ship in a parade?

   a **float** _____

4. What is a program about pretty ribbons?

   a **bow** _____

1 _____

2 _____

3 _____

4 _____

Find and circle four Spelling Words that are spelled wrong in these riddles. Then write each word correctly.

5. Why did the chicken cross the roade?

   to get to the other side

6. What kind of soup is in an artist's bole?

   doodle soup

7. What kind of bath can you take

   without sowp and water?

   a sunbath

8. What do you do if your owen tooth

   falls out?

   get toothpaste

5 _____

6 _____

7 _____

8 _____

Name _____

Words and More Words

Finish this puzzle. Write the noun from the box
that goes with each picture clue. You may need
to add **s** or **es**.

card	hat
brush	cup
watch	cake
box	bus
star	dish

Across

3.

5.

8.

10.

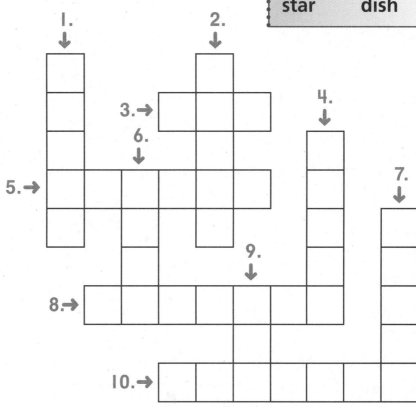

Down

1.

2.

4.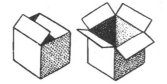

6.

7.

9.

Name _____

Dear Diary

Use the words below to complete Monday's diary entry. Then write a diary entry for Tuesday.

write   copied   matching   both

Monday

Today was my first day at school. My teacher wore a red dress

with _____ red shoes. Everyone thought she looked

so pretty.

I had to _____ a story. My friend Maria and I

_____ wrote about our black cats. It was just a

coincidence. But then Maria said that if I ever _____

her again, she would not be my dear friend.

Tuesday

_____

_____

_____

_____

Name

Why Be a Copycat?

Pretend you are Ruby. Complete the lines below to make a
poster that will help a new classmate make friends.

Miss Hart will

Angela will

The best way to make new friends is

Name _____

What If. . . and Then?

Pretend there is a new boy in your class. Write
possible causes and effects to complete the chart.

Cause	Effect
The new boy in your class can't find his pencil.	You
The boy	You offer to share your lunch with him.
The new boy gets lost trying to find the library.	You
The new boy	You ask the new boy to come over and play after school.

Finish this story.

Johanna gave Maria a present. Maria didn't like it. She _____

_____ .

Maria answered the telephone. It was Johanna. Before

Maria could say anything, Johanna said, " _____

_____ . "

Name

Hopping Around

Help Ruby's friends play Word Hopscotch. Each friend has chosen an **ou** word and will hop to words with the same sound. Write **ou** words in the boxes to match **ou** sounds on the shoes.

mouse	could	announced	ground
you	around	blouse	should

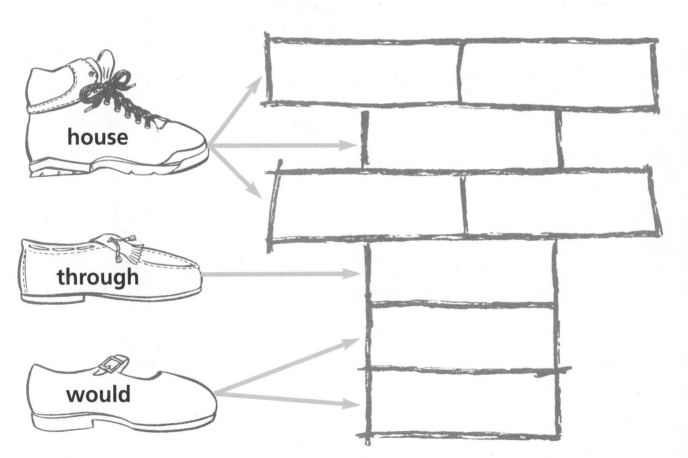

Now write a sentence using one of the words from the boxes.

_____

Name

Contraction Crossword

Write the contraction for each pair of words. The apostrophes are marked in the right places.

Across

2. are not

5. we are

6. I am

Down

1. you are

3. they will

4. she is

Pretend Ruby is giving Angela a hopping lesson. Write what each friend says. Use a contraction in each sentence.

Ruby says: "_____

_____"

Angela answers: "_____

_____"

Name

School Notes

Use the words from the box to finish Angela's note.

black	both
Dear	ever

_____ Ruby,

Why do you have to dress just like me? I wear a red bow.

Then you wear a red bow. I wear a _____

dress, so you wear one too. We _____ don't

always have to wear the same thing. Don't you

_____ think about wearing something just

because you like it?

Angela

Write Ruby's answer. Use the words **pretty** and **write**.

_____

_____

_____

_____

_____

_____

Name

What's Where?

Help Ruby finish the picture. Read and follow the directions.

1 Draw an apple on the desk.

2 Draw a clock by the door.

3 Draw a fish under the plant.

4 Draw a window at the left side of the classroom.

5 Draw a book on top of the bookshelf.

6 Draw a poster over the desk.

7 Tell where the boy will be if he walks backward.

_____

8 Tell where the girl will be if she walks forward.

_____

Name

A Web of Friends

Here is a simple web of friends
for **Ruby the Copycat**.

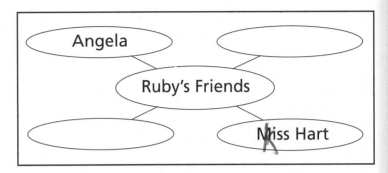

Angela

Ruby's Friends

Miss Hart

Friends may live far away or nearby.

Do you have friends who live far away? Write their names.

_____

One of Ruby's friends is her age. Another friend is a grownup.

Do you have friends of different ages? Write their names.

_____

What does friendship mean to you? Finish the sentence.

A friend is someone who _____

_____

Make **your** web of friends on another sheet of paper. Copy your
sentence about friendship at the top of the page.

Check your work.

☐ I showed friends who are near and far away and of
different ages.

☐ I wrote a sentence about friendship.

☐ I can explain why my friends are good friends.

MORE
SPELLING
PRACTICE

Contents

Pet Puzzles

These Spelling Words are words that you use in your writing. Look carefully at how they are spelled.

Use the Spelling Words to complete the sentences. Write the words in the puzzles.

Spelling Words

1. **the**	5. **you**
2. **will**	6. **said**
3. **have**	7. **it**
4. **was**	8. **they**

 Your Own Words

1. The pet show ____ start at noon.
2. Will your pet be in ____?
3. Who has ____ friendliest pet?
4. What kind of pet do you ____?
5. The parade of pets ____ the best event.
6. We ____, "We like the long-haired dog."
7. First, the dogs sat down, and then ____ rolled over.
8. Tell me which animal belongs to ____.

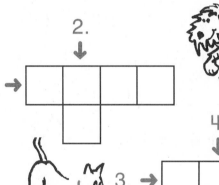

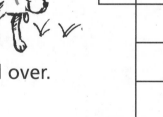

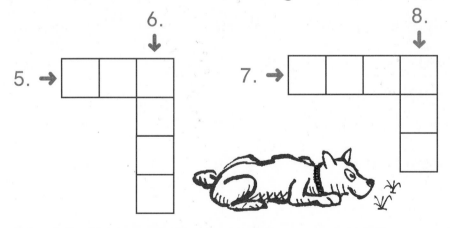

Which two Spelling Words begin like then?

9 _____   10 _____

SPELLING **Special Words**
for Writing

Name ....

Spelling Spree

Write the Spelling Word that completes each sentence.

Spelling Words	
1. **the**	5. **you**
2. **will**	6. **said**
3. **have**	7. **it**
4. **was**	8. **they**

1 Abby, how _____ you pick a name for your cat?

2 First, I _____ to see her play.

3 Then I am going to write _____ names I like best.

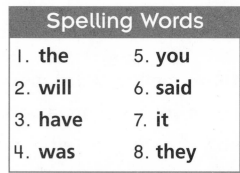

4 I will choose _____ from those names.

Find and circle four Spelling Words that are spelled wrong in this paragraph. Then write each word correctly.

   Nico could hardly wait. He wuz going with his big brother, Josh, to get a pet from the shelter. His mom and dad had saide that he could have a puppy, and thay were letting him pick it out today. Josh kept asking him, "What kind of dog do yoo want?"

5 _____

6 _____

7 _____

8 _____

Spelling Review

Write Spelling Words from the list
on this page to answer the questions.

Spelling Words	
thin	stay
when	them
such	left
she	chin

 Your Own Words

consonant clusters → slip   old
just   trip

1–2. Which two words have consonant clusters?

 1 _____   2 _____

the ch sound → chop   the sh sound → cash

3–4. Which two words begin or end with **ch**?

3 _____   4 _____

5. Which word begins with **sh**?

 5 _____

the th sound → thin that   the wh sound → white

6–7. Which two words begin with **th**?

6 _____   7 _____

8. Which word begins with **wh**?

 8 _____

Name

Spelling Spree

Think how the words in each group are alike. Write the missing Spelling Words. Use words from the list on this page.

Spelling Words	
said	dish
just	white
slip	was
will	you

1. cup, bowl, _____   ① _____

2. skid, trip, _____   ② _____

3. red, blue, _____   ③ _____

4. asked, yelled, _____   ④ _____

Find and circle four Spelling Words that are spelled wrong in this notice. Then write each word correctly.

Lost Dog

Has anyone seen my dog, Thor? She is a white boxer. Thor uas last seen on Pine Street. She wil be wearing a blue collar with tags. If yow find Thor, jus call my home at 555-6477. Please call soon. We miss her!

⑤ _____

⑥ _____

⑦ _____

⑧ _____

What's the Word?

These Spelling Words are words that you use in your writing. Look carefully at how they are spelled.

Use the Spelling Words to complete the sentences. Write the words in the bird feeder.

1. Do you ____ to feed birds?
2. It is not hard to do ____ you plan ahead.
3. Put a feeder on a porch or in a tree, and birds will ____ to it.
4. I ____ sure that you will be feeding something else too.
5. Watch closely ____ your window.
6. Mike looked out on ____ porch.
7. Julia saw something sitting on ____ feeder.
8. It had a bushy tail and ate seeds ____ top of the bird feeder.

Spelling Words

1. **on**
2. **am**
3. **if**
4. **from**

5. **his**
6. **her**
7. **come**
8. **want**

 Your Own Words

1 _____
2 _____
3 _____
4 _____
5 _____
6 _____
7 _____
8 _____

Which two Spelling Words have the short i sound?

9 _____

10 _____

Name

Spelling Spree

Write a Spelling Word to finish each riddle.
Can you name the animal in each one?

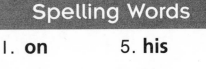

Spelling Words	
1. **on**	5. **his**
2. **am**	6. **her**
3. **if**	7. **come**
4. **from**	8. **want**

1 I _____ slow and live in a shell.
Sometimes you see me in a well.

2 I _____ peanuts to eat,
Bananas too, but never meat.

3 Maya had a pet with long ears.

It slept in _____ room for many years.

4 Ted took _____ pet for a walk.
It can say "Oink!" but cannot talk.

Find and circle four Spelling Words that are spelled wrong
in these instructions. Then write each word correctly.

Do you have seashells you want to
show off? First, get shells frum the
beach. Then put the shells awn a large
piece of paper. Next, write the name
of each shell next to the shell. Look in
a book about shells iff you need help.
Finally, ask your pals to com and see
your shells.

5 _____

6 _____

7 _____

8 _____

Answers: 1. turtle 2. monkey 3. rabbit 4. pig

Spelling Review

Write Spelling Words from the list on this page to answer the questions.

Spelling Words	
is	wind
jump	has
size	made
honk	job
nest	thing

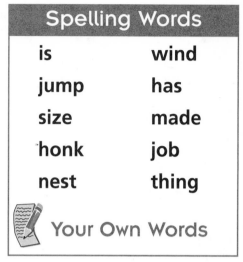

Your Own Words

the short a sound → ran
the short i sound → fish
the short u sound → cut
the short e sound → web
the short o sound → pod

1–5. Which letter spells the missing short vowel sound in each word? Write each word.

h ___ s   j ___ mp   n ___ st   j ___ b   ___ s

A long vowel sound may be spelled by the vowel-consonant-**e** pattern.
game   home   these   use   like

6–7. Which two words have a long vowel sound spelled by the vowel-consonant-**e** pattern? Draw a line under the letters that spell this pattern.

nd → sand   ng → sing   nk → thank

8–10. Which three words end with **nd, ng,** or **nk**?

1. _____
2. _____
3. _____
4. _____
5. _____
6. _____
7. _____
8. _____
9. _____
10. _____

Name _____

Spelling Spree

Write the Spelling Word that is the opposite of each word. Use words from the list on this page.

1 off _____

2 slow _____

3 float _____   **5** go _____

4 open _____   **6** those _____

Find and circle four Spelling Words that are spelled wrong in these instructions. Then write each word correctly.

How to Make a Bird Feeder

First, get an empty milk carton fram your home. Next, kut a hole near the bottom of the carton. Then push a small stick into a sput under the hole. Next, fill your feeder with birdseed. Finally, hang your feeder on a tree branch. If you waunt birds to keep coming, keep your feeder filled. The birds will thank you.

---

7 _____   **9** _____

8 _____   **10** _____

Name

At Camp

These Spelling Words are words that you use in your writing. Look carefully at how they are spelled.

Use the Spelling Words to complete the sentences. Write the words in the tents.

Spelling Words	
1. **of**	5. **time**
2. **do**	6. **went**
3. **to**	7. **what**
4. **name**	8. **been**

 Your Own Words

1. Last summer I ____ to camp.
2. I had a great ____ there.
3. Do you know ____ made camp fun?
4. I made friends with a girl whose ____ is Angie.
5. Angie was one ____ the campers in my cabin.
6. She also had never ____ to camp before.
7. We learned how ____ swim and use a boat.
8. There were so many interesting things to ____ !

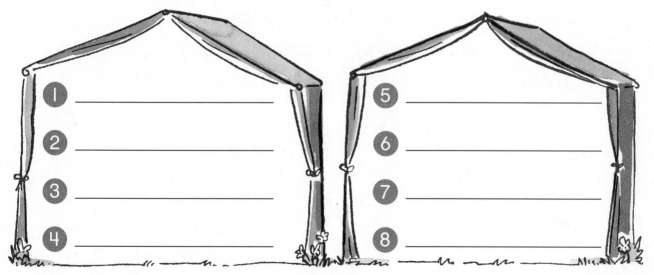

1. _____
2. _____
3. _____
4. _____

5. _____
6. _____
7. _____
8. _____

Which two Spelling Words end with a vowel sound?

9. _____   10. _____

Name _____

Spelling Spree

Find and circle four Spelling Words that are
spelled wrong in this letter. Then write each
word correctly.

Spelling Words	
1. **of**	5. **time**
2. **do**	6. **went**
3. **to**	7. **what**
4. **name**	8. **been**

Dear Anna,

    It has not ben a good day. I
whent to my new school. It was
raining. I fell in a puddle. Later, we
had a spelling test. I did not know any
ov the words. I want to go back to
my old school. What can I doo?

                    Your friend,
                    Sam

1 _____

2 _____

3 _____

4 _____

Write a Spelling Word for each clue. Then use the
letters from the boxes to find out what friends often
send each other.

5 something that everyone has ⬚ ___ ___ ___

6 the opposite of **from** ___ ⬚ ___ ___

7 a word that begins like **when** ___ ___ ___ ⬚

8 five o'clock ___ ___ ___ ⬚

Answer: a ___ ___ ___ ___

Spelling Review

Write Spelling Words from the list on this
page to answer the questions.

Spelling Words

show	road
way	you're
that's	team
see	own
sail	feed

 the long a sound ➝ pay, rain

1–2. Which two words have the long **a**
sound? Draw a line under the letters that
spell this sound.

✎ Your Own Words

 the long e sound ➝ need, speak

3–5. Which three words have the long **e** sound?
Draw a line under the letters that spell this
sound.

 the long o sound ➝ soap, bowl

6–8. Which three words have the long **o** sound?
Draw a line under the letters that spell this
sound.

 A **contraction** is a short way of saying
or writing two words.
do not ➝ don't   it is ➝ it's

9–10. What is the contraction for each pair of
words? Write the words.

    that is   you are

① _____

② _____

③ _____

④ _____

⑤ _____

⑥ _____

⑦ _____

⑧ _____

⑨ _____

⑩ _____

Name

Spelling Spree

Think how the words in each group are alike. Write the missing Spelling Words.

Spelling Words	
isn't	of
green	bowl
what	paint
coat	time
name	train

1 plate, cup, _____

2 red, yellow, _____

3 bus, car, _____

4 chalk, crayon, _____

5 hat, boots, _____

6 address, telephone number, _____

Find and circle four Spelling Words that are spelled wrong in this note. Then write each word correctly.

Dear Mia,

   Guess wat! Today I took my turtle, Sam, to school. We watched him crawl across the floor. He isnt very fast, so it took him a long tim. At lunch he ate some ov the lettuce I brought for him in a bowl. See you soon!

                               Your pal,
                               Ramón

7  _____   9  _____

8 _____   10  _____

Two Alike

Each Spelling Word is a homophone for another word on the list. **Homophones** are words that sound alike but do not have the same spelling or the same meaning.

 week   A **week** is an amount of time. One week is seven days.

 weak   **Weak** is the opposite of strong.

Write the Spelling Word that fits each clue. Then draw a circle around each pair of homophones.

1. I start on Sunday.
2. I cannot lift a big box.
3. I am another word for **important**.
4. I am found on the back of a horse's neck.
5. A cat or a dog has one.
6. I am a kind of story.
7. Use me when you dig up sand.
8. I am the opposite of **bright**.

1. _____
2. _____
3. _____
4. _____
5. _____
6. _____
7. _____
8. _____

Homophones

Homophones are words that sound alike but do not have the same spelling or the same meaning.

week   weak

Spelling Words

1. week
2. weak
3. pail
4. pale
5. tail
6. tale
7. main
8. mane

Challenge Words

1. blue
2. blew

My Study List
Add your own spelling words on the back. →

Take-Home Word Lists

My Study List

Name _____

1. _____

2. _____

3. _____

4. _____

5. _____

6. _____

7. _____

8. _____

Additional Spelling Words

1. see   3. so

2. sea   4. sew

How to Study a Word

LOOK at the word.

SAY the word.

THINK about the word.

WRITE the word.

CHECK the spelling.

150

Spelling Spree

Think how the words in each group are alike. Write the missing Spelling Words.

Spelling Words	
1. **week**	5. **tail**
2. **weak**	6. **tale**
3. **pail**	7. **main**
4. **pale**	8. **mane**

1. nose, paw, _____

2. day, month, _____

3. bucket, tub, _____

4. hoof, leg, _____

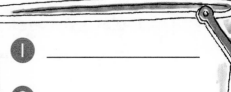

Find and circle four Spelling Words that are spelled wrong in this book report. Then write each word correctly.

<u>The Castaway</u> by Sam Bent is a true story, not a tail. A man was on a ship that sank. He swam to a land where no one lived. His mane food was coconuts. He got thin and pail. Each week he watched for a ship. At last he saw one. He was weke, but he swam to the ship and was saved.

5 _____   7 _____

6 _____   8 _____

150 More Spelling Practice

Name

Happy Puppy

Each Spelling Word has two parts, called **syllables**. Each syllable has one vowel sound. You hear the long **e** sound in the second syllable of each word. In these words, the long **e** sound is spelled **y**.

long e sound ➜ pup p**y**   par t**y**

Write the correct syllable from the bone to complete each Spelling Word.

1 pup _____

2 ba _____

3 po _____

4 dad _____

ly dy y py py by ny ty

5 par _____

6 hap _____

7 luck _____

8 sil _____

Now write each word. Draw a line under the letter that spells the long **e** sound in each word.

9 _____

10 _____

11 _____

12 _____

13 _____

14 _____

15 _____

16 _____

Take-Home Word Lists

Final Sound in **puppy**

long **e** sound ➜ **y**

pupp**y**   part**y**

Spelling Words

1. puppy
2. party
3. silly
4. pony
5. baby
6. lucky
7. happy
8. daddy

Challenge Words

1. noisy
2. furry

My Study List

Add your own spelling words on the back. ➜

Name _____

 My Study List

1. _____

2. _____

3. _____

4. _____

5. _____

6. _____

7. _____

8. _____

Additional Spelling Words

1. muddy   3. study

2. sticky   4. lady

How to Study a Word

LOOK at the word.

SAY the word.

THINK about the word.

WRITE the word.

CHECK the spelling.

152

Name _____

Spelling Spree

Spelling Words	
1. **puppy**	5. **baby**
2. **party**	6. **lucky**
3. **silly**	7. **happy**
4. **pony**	8. **daddy**

Write the Spelling Word that answers each question and rhymes with the word in **dark print**.

1 What is a thin horse? a **bony** _____

2 What is a bird with a prize? a _____ **ducky**

3 What is a foolish goat? a _____ **billy**

4 What is a glad father? a _____ **pappy**

Find and circle four Spelling Words that are spelled wrong in this part of a letter. Then write each word correctly.

Dear Josh,
    Yesterday Ellen put babe clothes on our pupy. She put a hat on his head. Then she sat him in a highchair. She said she was having a tea partey. She asked our dady and me to come. I felt so silly. It's hard to have a little sister!

5 _____   7 _____

6 _____   8 _____

152   **More Spelling Practice**

Name

Two Words in One

Each Spelling Word is a compound word.
A **compound word** is made up of two
shorter words.

mail + box = **mailbox**

Draw a line to connect the two words that
make up each Spelling Word. The first one is
done for you. Then write the Spelling Words.

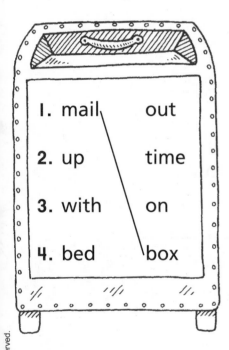

1. mail   out
2. up   time
3. with   on
4. bed   box

5. pan   paste
6. pea   cake
7. may   nut
8. tooth   be

1 _____

2 _____

3 _____

4 _____

5 _____

6 _____

7 _____

8 _____

Take-Home Word Lists

Compound Words

mail + box = **mailbox**

pea + nut = **peanut**

Spelling Words

1. mailbox
2. peanut
3. without
4. pancake
5. bedtime
6. maybe
7. upon
8. toothpaste

Challenge Words

1. sweatshirt
2. downstairs

My Study List

Add your own spelling

words on the back. →

Take-Home Word Lists

Name _____

My Study List

1. _____
2. _____
3. _____
4. _____
5. _____
6. _____
7. _____
8. _____

Additional Spelling Words

1. doghouse
2. backpack
3. footprint
4. grasshopper

How to Study a Word

LOOK at the word.

SAY the word.

THINK about the word.

WRITE the word.

CHECK the spelling.

154

Name _____

Spelling Spree

Write the Spelling Word for each clue.

Spelling Words

1. mailbox	5. bedtime
2. peanut	6. maybe
3. without	7. upon
4. pancake	8. toothpaste

1. You put me on your toothbrush.
2. I am good to eat for breakfast.
3. You make a kind of butter with me.
4. I mean "on top of."

1 _____   3 _____

2 _____   4 _____

Find and circle four Spelling Words that are spelled wrong in this ad. Then write each word correctly.

Kitty Cat Toothpaste

You always brush your teeth before bedtim. Why make your cat go witout brushing? Send us this ad to get a tube of toothpaste in your malbox. Then mabe your cat's teeth will shine!

5 _____   7 _____

6 _____   8 _____

154 More Spelling Practice

Learn to Earn

How to play

Players 2

You need

- list of Spelling Words
- blank cards
- green crayon

Getting ready

- Write a Spelling Word on each card. Color the back of each card green, and write **$1** on it.
- Stack the cards facedown.

Each player tries to earn the most money by spelling words correctly.

1. Player 1 takes a card and reads the word to Player 2.

2. Player 2 spells the word. If the spelling is correct, Player 1 gives the card to Player 2. If the spelling is wrong, Player 1 shows the correct spelling to Player 2 and puts the card facedown at the bottom of the stack.

3. Then Player 2 takes a card and reads the word to Player 1.

4. Players take turns spelling until there are no more cards in the stack. The player with the most money is the winner.

STAR SPELLER

How to play

Players 2

You need

- list of Spelling Words
- game board from page 157
- blank cards
- pencil
- 2 game markers

Getting ready

- Write a Spelling Word on each card. Beside each word write **1, 2,** or **3.**
- Stack the cards facedown. Place the markers at **Blast Off.**

Each player tries to be the first to complete the game by spelling words correctly.

1. Player 1 takes a card and reads the word to Player 2.

2. Player 2 spells the word. If the spelling is correct, Player 2 moves ahead on the board the number of spaces shown on the card.

3. If the spelling is not correct, Player 2 moves **back** the number of spaces shown on the card (except on the first turn).

4. After each turn, the card is placed facedown at the bottom of the stack.

5. Players take turns spelling words. The first player to reach **Finish** is the winner.

 # STAR SPELLER

FINISH

BLAST OFF!

Tick tack-Spell

How to play

Players 2 and a caller

You need

- list of Spelling Words
- paper
- 2 pencils of different colors

Getting ready

On a sheet of paper, draw lines for a ticktacktoe game. Draw two lines down and two lines across. (See the picture below.)

Each player tries to win the game by spelling words correctly and writing them in a row.

1. The caller reads a Spelling Word. Player 1 spells the word aloud.

2. Each player uses a different-colored pencil. If the word is spelled correctly, Player 1 writes it in a space. If the word is not spelled correctly, the caller spells it aloud correctly.

3. Players take turns spelling words. The first player to write words in three spaces in a row is the winner. (A row can be across, down, or from corner to corner.)

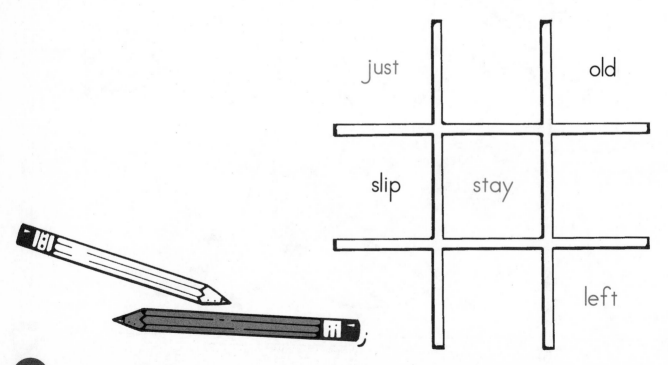

MY
HANDBOOK

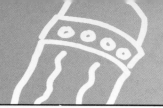

Contents

MY READING LOG

Use this log to record the books you read on your own.

Name of Book ______________________________

Author ______________________________

This book is about ______________________________

____

____

____

Name of Book ______________________________

Author ______________________________

This book is about ______________________________

____

____

____

Name of Book _____

Author _____

This book is about _____

_____

_____

_____

Name of Book _____

Author _____

This book is about _____

_____

_____

_____

Name of Book _____

Author _____

This book is about _____

_____

_____

_____

Name of Book _____

Author _____

This book is about _____

_____

_____

_____

Name of Book _____

Author _____

This book is about _____

_____

_____

_____

Name of Book _____

Author _____

This book is about _____

_____

_____

_____

Name of Book _____

Author _____

This book is about _____

_____

_____

_____

Name of Book _____

Author _____

This book is about _____

_____

_____

_____

Name of Book _____

Author _____

This book is about _____

_____

_____

_____

Trace and write the letters.

Aa Aa

Bb Bb

Cc Cc

Dd Dd

Ee Ee

Ff Ff

Gg Gg

HANDWRITING MODELS

Trace and write the letters.

Hh Hh

Ii Ii

Jj Jj

Kk Kk

Ll Ll

Mm Mm

McDougal, Littell 1993 Handwriting (continuous stroke)

Trace and write the letters.

Nn Nn

Oo Oo

Pp Pp

Qq Qq

Rr Rr

Ss Ss

Tt Tt

McDougal, Littell 1993 Handwriting (continuous stroke)

HANDWRITING MODELS

Trace and write the letters.

Uu Uu

Vv Vv

Ww Ww

Xx Xx

Yy Yy

Zz Zz

McDougal, Littell 1993 Handwriting (continuous stroke)

HANDWRITING MODELS

Trace and write the letters.

Aa Aa

Bb Bb

Cc Cc

Dd Dd

Ee Ee

Ff Ff

Gg Gg

HANDWRITING MODELS

Trace and write the letters.

Hh Hh

Ii Ii

Jj Jj

Kk Kk

Ll Ll

Mm Mm

McDougal, Littell 1990 Handwriting (ball and stick)

Trace and write the letters.

Nn Nn

Oo Oo

Pp Pp

Qq Qq

Rr Rr

Ss Ss

Tt Tt

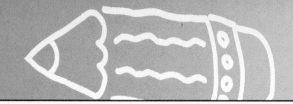

Trace and write the letters.

Uu Uu

Vv Vv

Ww Ww

Xx Xx

Yy Yy

Zz Zz

McDougal, Littell 1990 Handwriting (ball and stick)

How to Study a Word

1 LOOK at the word.
- What does the word mean?
- What letters are in the word?
- Name and touch each letter.

2 SAY the word.
- Listen for the consonant sounds.
- Listen for the vowel sounds.

3 THINK about the word.
- How is each sound spelled?
- Close your eyes and picture the word.
- What other words have the same spelling patterns?

4 WRITE the word.
- Think about the sounds and the letters.
- Form the letters correctly.

5 CHECK the spelling.
- Did you spell the word the same way it is spelled in your word list?
- Write the word again if you did not spell it correctly.

SPECIAL WORDS FOR WRITING

A
about
again
a lot
always
am
and
any
are
around
as

B
back
because
been
before

C
cannot
caught
come
coming
could

D
do
does

done
down

E
enough

F
family
first
for
found
friend
from

G
getting
girl
goes
going

H
has
have
heard
her
here
his
how

I
I'd
if
I'll
I'm
into
it
it's

K
knew
know

L
letter
little

M
many
more
my
myself

N
name
never
new
now

O
of
off
on
once
one
other
our
outside

P
people
pretty

R
really
right

S
said
school
some
something
started
stopped

T
that's
the
their
there

they
thought
through
time
to
today
too
tried
two

V
very

W
want
was
went
were
what
when
where
who
will
would
write

Y
you
your

Arthur's Pet Business

Words with

sh **or** ch

sh sound ➞ **sh**e, di**sh**

ch sound ➞ **ch**in, mu**ch**

Spelling Words

1. dish
2. she
3. much
4. cash
5. chin
6. wish
7. such
8. chop

Challenge Words

1. brush
2. leash

My Study List

Add your own spelling words on the back. ➞

The Cats of Tiffany Street

Consonant Clusters

ju**st**   **l**e**ft**

drove   o**ld**

glad

Spelling Words

1. left
2. just
3. stay
4. old
5. slip
6. drove
7. trip
8. glad

Challenge Words

1. climb
2. floor

My Study List

Add your own spelling words on the back. ➞

Name _____

 My Study List

1. _____

2. _____

3. _____

4. _____

5. _____

6. _____

7. _____

8. _____

Additional Spelling Words

1. lost   **3.** help

2. swim   **4.** milk

How to Study a Word

LOOK at the word.

SAY the word.

THINK about the word.

WRITE the word.

CHECK the spelling.

Name _____

 My Study List

1. _____

2. _____

3. _____

4. _____

5. _____

6. _____

7. _____

8. _____

Additional Spelling Words

1. wash   **3.** each

2. sheep   **4.** chase

How to Study a Word

LOOK at the word.

SAY the word.

THINK about the word.

WRITE the word.

CHECK the spelling.

Julius

Pet Show Today!: Reading-Writing Workshop

Words with

th **or** wh

th sounds → **th**at, **th**in

wh sound → **wh**en

Look carefully at how these words are spelled.

Spelling Words

1. that
2. them
3. when
4. with
5. than
6. white
7. thin
8. which

Challenge Words

1. think
2. where

Spelling Words

1. the
2. will
3. have
4. was
5. you
6. said
7. it
8. they

Challenge Words

1. because
2. family

My Study List

Add your own spelling words on the back. →

My Study List

Add your own spelling words on the back. →

Name _____

 My Study List

1. _____

2. _____

3. _____

4. _____

5. _____

6. _____

7. _____

8. _____

Additional Spelling Words

1. as   **3.** off

2. my   **4.** any

How to Study a Word

LOOK at the word.

SAY the word.

THINK about the word.

WRITE the word.

CHECK the spelling.

178

Name _____

 My Study List

1. _____

2. _____

3. _____

4. _____

5. _____

6. _____

7. _____

8. _____

Additional Spelling Words

1. why   **3.** teeth

2. then   **4.** what

How to Study a Word

LOOK at the word.

SAY the word.

THINK about the word.

WRITE the word.

CHECK the spelling.

178

Animal Tracks

Short Vowels

short **a** sound → r**a**n

short **i** sound → **i**s

short **u** sound → m**u**d

Spelling Words

1. mud
2. is
3. ran
4. has
5. jump
6. fast
7. cut
8. fish

Challenge Words

1. tracks
2. until

My Study List

Add your own spelling words
on the back. →

Pet Show Today!: Spelling Review

Spelling Words

1. thin
2. when
3. such
4. she
5. stay
6. them
7. left
8. chin
9. said
10. just
11. slip
12. will
13. dish
14. white
15. was
16. you

**See the back for
Challenge Words.**

My Study List

Add your own spelling words
on the back. →

Name_____

My Study List

1. _____
2. _____
3. _____
4. _____
5. _____
6. _____
7. _____
8. _____

Challenge Words

1. think   **3.** leash

2. floor   **4.** family

How to Study a Word

LOOK at the word.

SAY the word.

THINK about the word.

WRITE the word.

CHECK the spelling.

Name_____

My Study List

1. _____
2. _____
3. _____
4. _____
5. _____
6. _____
7. _____
8. _____

Additional Spelling Words

1. plant   **3.** fix

2. duck   **4.** flat

How to Study a Word

LOOK at the word.

SAY the word.

THINK about the word.

WRITE the word.

CHECK the spelling.

What Lives in a Shell?

Vowel-Consonant-e Spellings

long **a** sound → m**a**d**e**
long **e** sound → th**ese**
long **i** sound → l**ike**
long **o** sound → cl**ose**
long **u** sound → **use**

Spelling Words

1. home
2. game
3. made
4. use
5. close
6. like
7. size
8. these

Challenge Words

1. inside
2. race

My Study List

Add your own spelling words on the back. →

Nature Spy

More Short Vowels

short **e** sound → w**e**b
short **o** sound → r**o**ck

Spelling Words

1. web
2. rock
3. nest
4. pod
5. spot
6. leg
7. pet
8. job

Challenge Words

1. shell
2. else

My Study List

Add your own spelling words on the back. →

Name_____

 My Study List

1. _____

2. _____

3. _____

4. _____

5. _____

6. _____

7. _____

8. _____

Additional Spelling Words

1. pond   **3.** sock

2. neck   **4.** spell

How to Study a Word

LOOK at the word.

SAY the word.

THINK about the word.

WRITE the word.

CHECK the spelling.

Name_____

 My Study List

1. _____

2. _____

3. _____

4. _____

5. _____

6. _____

7. _____

8. _____

Additional Spelling Words

1. ate   **3.** wide

2. fine   **4.** note

How to Study a Word

LOOK at the word.

SAY the word.

THINK about the word.

WRITE the word.

CHECK the spelling.

Where Does the Trail Lead?

> **Words That End with**
>
> nd, ng, **or** nk
>
> nd   →   a**nd**
>
> ng   →   thi**ng**
>
> nk   →   si**nk**

Spelling Words

1. sand
2. sink
3. and
4. wind
5. honk
6. thing
7. thank
8. sing

Challenge Words

1. along
2. among

My Study List

Add your own spelling words on the back.   →

Be a Nature Detective: Reading-Writing Workshop

> Look carefully at how these words are spelled.

Spelling Words

1. on
2. am
3. if
4. from
5. his
6. her
7. come
8. want

Challenge Words

1. really
2. caught

My Study List

Add your own spelling words on the back.   →

Name _____

 My Study List

1. _____

2. _____

3. _____

4. _____

5. _____

6. _____

7. _____

8. _____

Additional Spelling Words

1. does   **3.** their

2. goes   **4.** there

How to Study a Word

LOOK at the word.

SAY the word.

THINK about the word.

WRITE the word.

CHECK the spelling.

Name _____

 My Study List

1. _____

2. _____

3. _____

4. _____

5. _____

6. _____

7. _____

8. _____

Additional Spelling Words

1. bend   **3.** hand

2. sting   **4.** junk

How to Study a Word

LOOK at the word.

SAY the word.

THINK about the word.

WRITE the word.

CHECK the spelling.

My First American Friend

> ### More Long a Spellings
>
> long **a** sound ➜ pl**ay**
>
> ➜ tr**ai**n

Spelling Words

1. train
2. play
3. day
4. paint
5. way
6. rain
7. sail
8. pay

Challenge Words

1. always
2. afraid

Be a Nature Detective: Spelling Review

Spelling Words

1. is
2. jump
3. size
4. honk
5. nest
6. wind
7. has
8. made
9. job
10. thing
11. sink
12. come
13. from
14. on
15. close
16. spot
17. fast
18. want
19. cut
20. these

See the back for Challenge Words.

My Study List

Add your own spelling words on the back. ➜

My Study List

Add your own spelling words on the back. ➜

Name_____

 My Study List

1. _____

2. _____

3. _____

4. _____

5. _____

6. _____

7. _____

8. _____

Challenge Words

1. among   **4.** tracks

2. shell   **5.** inside

3. caught

How to Study a Word

LOOK at the word.

SAY the word.

THINK about the word.

WRITE the word.

CHECK the spelling.

Name_____

 My Study List

1. _____

2. _____

3. _____

4. _____

5. _____

6. _____

7. _____

8. _____

Additional Spelling Words

1. stain   **3.** wait

2. pray   **4.** lay

How to Study a Word

LOOK at the word.

SAY the word.

THINK about the word.

WRITE the word.

CHECK the spelling.

Good Friends: Reading-Writing Workshop

Look carefully at how these words are spelled.

Spelling Words

1. of
2. do
3. to
4. name
5. time
6. went
7. what
8. been

Challenge Words

1. right
2. thought

My Study List

Add your own spelling words on the back. →

Watch Out, Ronald Morgan!

More Long e **Spellings**

long **e** sound → s**ee**

→ r**ea**d

Spelling Words

1. see
2. read
3. need
4. please
5. team
6. green
7. speak
8. feed

Challenge Words

1. sneakers
2. agree

My Study List

Add your own spelling words on the back. →

Name_____

 My Study List

1. _____
2. _____
3. _____
4. _____
5. _____
6. _____
7. _____
8. _____

Additional Spelling Words

1. cheat   **3.** street

2. sweep   **4.** leave

How to Study a Word

LOOK at the word.

SAY the word.

THINK about the word.

WRITE the word.

CHECK the spelling.

Name_____

 My Study List

1. _____
2. _____
3. _____
4. _____
5. _____
6. _____
7. _____
8. _____

Additional Spelling Words

1. write   **3.** too

2. myself   **4.** little

How to Study a Word

LOOK at the word.

SAY the word.

THINK about the word.

WRITE the word.

CHECK the spelling.

Ruby the Copycat

What Kind of Baby-sitter Is This?

Contractions

do not	→	**don't**
we will	→	**we'll**
you are	→	**you're**

More Long o
Spellings

long **o** sound	→	s**o**ap
	→	**o**wn

Spelling Words

1. I'm
2. don't
3. it's
4. didn't
5. that's
6. we'll
7. isn't
8. you're

Spelling Words

1. own
2. soap
3. coat
4. show
5. bowl
6. slow
7. road
8. boat

Challenge Words

1. who's
2. wouldn't

Challenge Words

1. know
2. tomorrow

My Study List

Add your own spelling words on the back. ⟶

My Study List

Add your own spelling words on the back. ⟶

Name _____

 My Study List

1. _____

2. _____

3. _____

4. _____

5. _____

6. _____

7. _____

8. _____

Additional Spelling Words

1. goat   **3.** grow

2. low   **4.** toast

How to Study a Word

LOOK at the word.

SAY the word.

THINK about the word.

WRITE the word.

CHECK the spelling.

Name _____

 My Study List

1. _____

2. _____

3. _____

4. _____

5. _____

6. _____

7. _____

8. _____

Additional Spelling Words

1. she'll   **3.** can't

2. I've   **4.** what's

How to Study a Word

LOOK at the word.

SAY the word.

THINK about the word.

WRITE the word.

CHECK the spelling.

Good Friends: Spelling Review

Spelling Words

1. show	11. isn't
2. way	12. green
3. that's	13. what
4. see	14. coat
5. sail	15. name
6. road	16. of
7. you're	17. bowl
8. team	18. paint
9. own	19. time
10. feed	20. train

See the back for Challenge Words.

My Study List

Add your own spelling words on the back. ⟶

Name_____

 My Study List

1. _____

2. _____

3. _____

4. _____

5. _____

6. _____

7. _____

8. _____

Challenge Words

1. always   **4.** know

2. right   **5.** who's

3. agree

How to Study a Word

LOOK at the word.

SAY the word.

THINK about the word.

WRITE the word.

CHECK the spelling.

1 A short vowel sound may be spelled **a, e, i, o,** or **u**.

hat	top
pet	fun
pin	

2 Two consonant sounds said close together may be spelled **st, tr, dr, gl, ft, sl,** or **ld**.

star	**gl**ad
ju**st**	le**ft**
trip	**sl**ip
drove	o**ld**

3 The sound that begins **show** may be spelled **sh**, and the sound that ends **much** may be spelled **ch**.

she	**ch**in
wi**sh**	mu**ch**

4 The sound that begins **when** may be spelled **wh**. The sounds that begin **thin** and **that** are both spelled **th**.

what	with
there	

5 The long **a** sound may be spelled **ai, ay,** or **a**-consonant-**e**.

tr**ai**n	m**a**d**e**
pl**ay**	g**a**m**e**

6 The long **e** sound may be spelled **ee, ea,** or **e**-consonant-**e**.

t**ea**m	n**ee**d
r**ea**d	th**e**s**e**

7 The long **o** sound may be spelled **oa, ow,** or **o**-consonant-**e**.

c**oa**t	h**o**m**e**
sl**ow**	

8 The long **i** sound may be spelled **i**-consonant-**e**.

size　**like**

9 The long **u** sound may be spelled **u**-consonant-**e**.

use　**cute**

10 Words that end with **nd** have both the **n** and **d** sounds.

sa**nd**　**and**

11 In words that end with **ng** or **nk**, you may not hear the **n** sound.

thi**ng**　ho**nk**

12 In **contractions**, an apostrophe takes the place of a missing letter or letters.

you're　we'll
it's　don't

13 Add **s** to most words to mean more than one. When a word ends with **s, x, sh,** or **ch,** add **es** to name more than one.

coat**s**　wi**shes**
bus**es**　pea**ches**
bo**xes**

14 The final **e** in some words is dropped before adding **ed** or **ing**.

shar**ed**　tak**ing**

15 The final consonant in some words is doubled before adding **ed** or **ing**.

stop**ped**　hug**ging**

16 The vowel sound in **ball** may be spelled **aw** or **a** before **ll.**

saw   call

17 The vowel sound in **boy** may be spelled **oi** or **oy**.

oil   joy

18 The vowel sound in **cow** may be spelled **ow** or **ou**.

do**w**n   mo**u**se

19 The vowel + **r** sounds may be spelled **ar, or, ore,** or **er**.

arm   st**ore**
b**or**n   ov**er**

20 The vowel sound in **moon** may be spelled **oo**.

r**oo**m   s**oo**n

21 The vowel sound in **book** may be spelled **oo**.

f**oo**t   l**oo**k

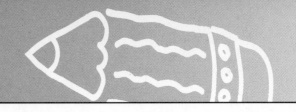

Grammar, Capitalization, and Punctuation

SENTENCES

A **sentence** tells what someone or something did.

We ate dinner.   The boy rode the bus.

Kinds of Sentences

A **telling sentence** tells something. It begins with a capital letter.
It ends with a period.

The horse won the race.   Cathy went to the store.

A **question** asks something. It begins with a capital letter.
It ends with a question mark.

Are you hungry?   Do you like to play soccer?

An **exclamation** shows strong feeling. It begins with a capital letter.
It ends with an exclamation point.

I loved that book!   What a fun day that was!

Naming Parts and Action Parts

Every sentence has a **naming part** and an **action part.**

The **naming part** of a sentence tells who or what.

Jennifer played in the snow.   **The sky** looks beautiful today.

The **action part** of a sentence tells what is happening.

> The train **moves fast.**   Alex **laughs.**

NOUNS

A **noun** names a person, a place, or a thing.

> The **girl** likes to run.   We saw the **pig**.
> Shelley went to the **park**.

Special Nouns

Some nouns name special people, places, or things.

These **special nouns** begin with capital letters.

Nouns	Special Nouns
My **dog** loves to play.	**Fluffy** loves to play.
The **park** is her favorite place.	**Jefferson Park** is her favorite place.

Nouns for One and More Than One

A noun can name one person, place, or thing.

> Tommy picked up the **cat**.   She walked by the **tree**.

A noun can also name more than one person, place, or thing.

> Tommy picked up the **cats**.   She walked by the **trees**.

Add **s** to most nouns to name more than one.

> The rug**s** were wet. The hat**s** were silly.

Add **es** to nouns that end with **s, x, ch,** and **sh**
to name more than one.

> These glass**es** are old. The watch**es** need to be fixed.
>
> The fox**es** were playing. The dish**es** are dry.

A few nouns change their spelling to name more than one.

> one child ➤ two child**ren** one man ➤ two m**en**
>
> one foot ➤ two f**ee**t one woman ➤ two wom**en**

PRONOUNS

A **pronoun** can take the place of a noun.

He, she, it, and **they** are pronouns.

> **Karen** likes to swim. **She** likes to swim.
>
> **Brett** likes to swim too. **He** likes to swim too.
>
> **Maria and Brett** meet Karen **They** meet Karen at the pool.
> at the pool.
>
> **The water** is very warm. **It** is very warm.

VERBS

A **verb** names an action.

> Mary **plays** the piano beautifully.
>
> The birds **fly** over the trees.
>
> The baby **drinks** the juice.
>
> I **get** my lunch.

Verbs That Tell About Now

A verb can tell about an action that is happening now.

Add **s** to a verb that tells about one.

> The cat **plays** with the ball.   Tricia **smiles**.

Do not add **s** to a verb that tells about more than one.

> The boys **sing** songs.

Verbs That Tell About the Past

A verb can name actions that happened before now, or in the past.

Add **ed** to a verb to show that something happened in the past.

> We **walked** to the store.
>
> Marta **called** her on the phone.
>
> Kim **rowed** the boat to safety.

Is, Are, Was, Were

Is and **are** tell about something that is happening **now**.

Use **is** with one. Use **are** with more than one.

Mr. Roberts **is** my teacher.   They **are** at home.

Was and **were** tell about something that happened in the past.

I **was** at the party yesterday.   My friends **were** already there.

Irregular Verbs

Some special verbs change spelling to tell about the past.

Have and **Do**

William **has** fun at the fair.   He **does** like hats.

People **have** fun at the fair.   They **do** like hats.

They **had** fun at the fair.   She **did** like hats.

Take and **Make**

He **takes** some cookies.   He **makes** toys.

They **take** some cookies.   The girls **make** toys.

We **took** some cookies.   Everyone **made** toys.

Throw and **Break**

Jimmy **throws** the ball.   The man **breaks** the glass.

The players **throw** the ball.   The workers **break** the glass.

Kara **threw** the ball.   The dog **broke** the glass.

ADJECTIVES

An **adjective** is a word that tells how something looks, feels, tastes, smells, and sounds.

The **pretty** sunset made them happy. (looks)

The child was sleeping in a **soft** blanket. (feels)

The pizza was **spicy**. (tastes)

Many flowers have a **sweet** smell. (smells)

The **loud** siren scared her. (sounds)

Adjectives can also tell size, shape, color, and how many.

The **large** cloud moved slowly. (size)

The child had a **round** face.   (shape)

The **blue** hat is in the box. (color)

Two workers walked into the building. (how many)

Comparing with Adjectives

Add **er** to adjectives to compare two people, places, or things.

Lupe had **shorter** hair than Kelly.

Add **est** to compare more than two people, places, or things.

Lee had the **shortest** hair in the class.

CAPITALIZATION

Every sentence begins with a capital letter.

The weather is sunny.

The names of the days of the week begin with capital letters.

The party is on **T**uesday.

The names of months begin with capital letters.

We go camping every year in **A**ugust.

The names of holidays begin with capital letters.

I want to buy my mother a **M**other's **D**ay gift.

A title begins with a capital letter.

Put a period after **Mrs.**, **Mr.**, **Ms.**, and **Dr.**

The title **Miss** does not have a period.

Mrs. Jackson	**Ms.** Sloane	**Dr.** Lee
Mr. Fernandez	**Miss** Jones	

The first word, the last word, and each important word in a book title begin with a capital letter. Book titles are underlined.

I like the book <u>**B**ringing the **R**ain to **K**apiti **P**lain</u>.

PUNCTUATION

Ending Sentences

A telling sentence ends with a period.

All of Timmy's friends will be at the party**.**

A question ends with a question mark.

Will there be balloons and cake at the party**?**

An exclamation ends with an exclamation point.

That cake was really good**!**

Contractions

Use an apostrophe in contractions to take the place of missing letters.

isn't (is not)	it's (it is)
can't (cannot)	I'm (I am)
wouldn't (would not)	they've (they have)
wasn't (was not)	they'll (they will)
we're (we are)	you're (you are)

Comma

Use a comma between the day and the year in dates.

My sister was born August 22**,** 1995.

Use a comma between the name of a city and the name of a state.

We went on a trip to Phoenix**,** Arizona.

Her family lives in San Jose**,** California.

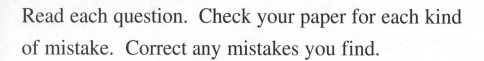

Read each question. Check your paper for each kind of mistake. Correct any mistakes you find.

- ☐ Did I begin each sentence with a capital letter?
- ☐ Did I use the correct end mark?
- ☐ Did I spell each word correctly?
- ☐ Did I indent each paragraph?

PROOFREADING MARKS

Mark	Meaning	Example
∧	Add one or more words.	I ∧ see the play. *(want to)*
—	Take out one or more words.	The boat ~~did~~ moved slowly.
—	Change the spelling.	The cloud ~~filed~~ *(filled)* the sky.
/	Make a capital letter a small letter.	The A/nimals hid from the storm.
=	Make a small letter a capital letter.	There are thirty days in april.